Life-Styled Marketing

Life-Styled Marketing

How to Position Products for Premium Profits

REVISED EDITION

MACK HANAN

amacom

A Division of American Management Associations

Library of Congress Cataloging in Publication Data

Hanan, Mack.
  Life-styled marketing.

  Includes index.
  1. Marketing. 2. New products. I. Title.
HF5415.H1863 1980   658.8   79-54833
ISBN 0-8144-5567-0

© 1972, 1980 AMACOM
A division of American Management Associations, New York.
Printed in the United States of America.

First Printing

1 /9723 9/15/81

To Peter Karp

*Whom I would have had to invent
if he had not existed*

*When I made my
first tentative steps
into other people's life-styles*

*And needed a creative companion,
a resonant sounding board,
and the supplemental faith to
hang in.*

Foreword to the Revised Edition

If you want to run up superior profits in your business, there are two ways you can go. First, you can manipulate your organization by spinning out a subsidiary or a division into a free-standing company, by starting new business ventures, and by making acquisitions. Or you can manipulate your operations, especially R&D and marketing.

You can get dual leverage out of R&D and marketing. Developing and marketing new products is one way to earn growth profits. Repositioning some of your established products to make them "new" is another way. Both of these operational strategies have the ability to produce the marketer's most desired outcome: to provide you with the opportunity to command premium price.

Premium price is central to business growth. It is the cause of premium profit. At the same time, it is the result of offering premium values. Since profit flows from price and since price flows from value, the bottom-line question we all have to answer is, *How can new products and established products be positioned to deliver the highest perceived values?*

On the face of it, the question seems simple enough. Yet in the course of answering it, untold millions of dollars have gone down the drain. Historically, positioning products for premium price has been a failure-ridden enterprise. It is not because companies have failed to understand *what* to put into new or repositioned products. Far more often, they have lacked the skill of seizing the concept of their markets—that is, of knowing how to make their products necessary by integrating the values they offer into the life-style values of their markets.

How can this be the case when there are so many ways of classifying markets (demographics, psychographics, needs analysis, product-preference profiles—no one really knows them all)? When we are so inundated with methods of cutting into a market, who needs one more way?

At least four kinds of marketers share this need: All consumer product marketers, all suppliers of consumer and professional services, many high-technology manufacturers, and some industrial manufacturers can substantially improve their profit pictures when they start to base product positioning on customer or consumer life-styles. How do we know? Because they already have gained significant new profits through life-styling and they continue to bring them home.

As a direct result of life-styling, a broad spectrum of life-styled products and services have provided their marketers with superior revenues: packaged foods, soft drinks, beer, ethical drugs, health and beauty aids, personal care products and services, home appliances and entertainment products, home education products and services, travel services, insurance, financial services, communications and telecommunications systems, office equipment and systems, hydraulic transmission systems, and many others.

Why does life-styling work, often spectacularly and

even after traditional market-seizing approaches have produced only "me, too" commodity positionings for products and services that deserved better? Life-styling does something none of the other strategies do: *it forces the market into a product's marketing even before the product is brought out to the market.*

As we practice life-styling, we do more than simply study a market's attitude and activity patterns that define its main use situations. We live them along with the market itself. We share its problems. We test out its remedies and solutions. We think through the rational aspects of its needs and empathize with the emotional feelings that attend them. We do not ask markets what they think or want; we think the same thoughts and feel the same wants because we ourselves have become the market. We have not just lived *with* them. We have lived *as* them—a far cry from being visiting professors *of* them.

Life-styled marketing allows marketers to live as their markets live in the key areas of their product use so that their product positionings can be made to match even before they are put up for sale.

It is difficult to know who is most appreciative of marketing in a life-styled manner. Marketing and sales managers, research and development managers who use life-styling to create highly commercial new products, market research managers, advertising and sales promotion managers, venture business managers, corporate development managers and corporate planners, and financial managers who enjoy beefed-up profits—all of these functional specialists have been placing a high value on life-styling. So have the people who comprise their markets and who show their appreciation by paying premium prices for products that have added significant new values to their lives.

Mack Hanan

Contents

1

Introduction to Life-Styled Marketing

For a company whose objective is to grow and diversify the base of its business, new product development almost always seems to be the least of three evils. It is a good deal more familiar than branching out into totally new businesses. And most of the time it is financially, legally, and organizationally less formidable than merger and acquisition. Yet familiar or not, failure rather than success is implicit in the introduction of new products and services. It has become something of a game to speculate on the rate of new product failure at figures ranging anywhere from 90 percent downward, depending on the developer's definition of "new," "product," and "failure." But persistent inquiry makes it seem clear that somewhere between one-fourth and one-third of major new products introduced over the past five years have admittedly failed to meet their developers' objectives. How many other innovative product or service concepts fail in the creative or evaluative stage—or never make it out of test marketing—is unknowable. In most of these cases of failure, the major reason acknowledged by their developers is virtually the same: *inadequate appraisal of the market,* which has prevented the developer from properly seizing its needs and has resulted in seriously misjudging the number of customers prepared to accept what he had to offer.

New product developers who work with a well-conceived visualization of their market can be as much as two-thirds of the way home before they start to innovate. This is why the lowest risk for product developers is always in the area of creating new products for their existing markets—their key accounts or hard-core purchasers who represent the 20 percent of their customers responsible for providing up to 80 percent of their profitable sales volume. It is also the reason why the second lowest area of risk is product development for markets whose composition and needs are closely adjacent to a company's existing markets. The more remote a market is from the new product developer's conception, the greater the risk.

What Life-Styled Marketing Is

The productivity of the development function for most companies can therefore almost always be increased by a strategy that assigns priority to defining, understanding, and serving existing markets first of all, adjacent markets second, and new markets last. What is required is an approach that can accomplish three things: (1) encourage existing markets to reveal more of their needs than are now being served and to reveal known needs more meaningfully; (2) allow adjacent markets to disclose needs similar to those which are now being served in existing markets; and (3) enable new markets to be seen in terms of their familiarity to existing markets rather than their strangeness. One such approach that can help many new product developers achieve these objectives more predictably is *life-styled marketing, a strategy for seizing the con-*

cept of a market according to its most meaningful, recurrent patterns of attitudes and activities, and then tailoring products and their promotional strategies to fit these patterns.

A Systems Approach

Life-styled marketing—marketing to the needs contained in a style of consumer or business life—is a systems approach to conceiving a market. It is concerned with the patterns of activities that recur most frequently among a customer group, looking for expressions of ways of coping with important aspects of life that culminate in heavy purchases. And at the same time, it identifies the thought patterns and self-images that accompany these activities so that they can be efficiently promoted to.

Within each pattern of attitudes and activities, the life-styling developer looks for three major attributes of each market group:

1. Its *psychographics,* expressed by its major needs that seek commercial benefits along with its primary personality characteristics, its commercial behavior, and its apparent value systems.
2. Its *product usage* and *media usage* habits, especially the ways in which it perceives and evaluates the various product and media categories it consumes.
3. Its *demographics,* such as age, education, and income.

For a health and beauty aids manufacturer, one important pattern of attitudes and activities in his existing market can be called a woman homemaker's life-style role as "family physician." In this role, the homemaker is acting, thinking, and feeling like a nonprofessional practitioner of nursing and medical functions. Many of her concerns are the same as those shared by medical doctors and registered nurses in a hospital environment, but because she is in the home, she must deprofessionalize these concerns. Profitable new product opportunities exist for health and beauty aids developers who can commercialize her needs within the context of this life-style role—who can, in other words, get inside the role with her, act it out and emotionalize it with her, and look for commercial opportunities in health care products and information services that otherwise they might not have seen as vividly or as systematically.

This same concept of a market—the life-style role of family physician—can also be useful to new product developers who work from a vastly different base than health and beauty capabilities. Food processing developers, for example, are accustomed to relating to their market of women homemakers in their roles as "family dietitians." When many of these same women are newly considered in the light of their physician-in-the-home life-styles, product ideas can be generated in functional foods that also contain a health or nutritional market benefit. This approach can yield seasonal foods to prevent winter health problems, foods designed for people who are recovering from major illnesses, foods that provide quick energy, or foods that give added values to people when they need to react under stress. In a similar manner, new product developers for insurance companies or for furniture or disposable-apparel manufacturers can utilize the family physician life-style as a market base.

Industrial manufacturers and service suppliers can also style their markets according to patterns of attitudes and activities. An airline, for example, can apply new-service thinking to its basic market of business executives in their styles of life as commercial airline travelers, corporate aircraft buyers, and vacation trip planners. Many of these same businesspeople are also the prime market targets for a business publisher, who meets their life-styled needs for information services. For each major aspect of their life-styled roles which can be identified, the developer may be able to introduce a marketable service along lines such as these that have been worked out with Gordon Jones (on behalf of McGraw-Hill) to serve business managers in their roles as problem solvers:

Aspects of Problem Solver Life-style Role	*Potential Commercial Services*
Learner and applier of instant information	Weekly newsletter or cassette
Learner and applier of information in depth	Monthly magazines, books, and information centers
Learner and applier of specific problem-solving information and expertise	Educational seminars and consultation services

In this book, we will be dealing with a variety of lifestyles for men and women customers of consumer and industrial businesses: *men* in their professional roles of problem solvers, corporate travel managers, and materials handling managers, and in their personal roles of "swingers" and "easy rider multistylists"; *women* as family physicians, dietitians, internal environment creators and managers, as well as new roles that were once the exclusive preserve of men. Life-styled marketing approaches to these roles can give the product developer an intimate orientation to his market that no statistical description of its demographics and no mere itemization of a single major need can provide. By life-styling a market, the developer can construct an operating model of its attitude and activity processes that his marketing and technical capabilities can serve. By constructing models of the market's relevant life-styles, the developer can move inside them and live them out by rehearsing their events which inspire new product requirements. This gives the developer the chance to do more than just *know* his market; it virtually permits him to *become* the market by replicating its living patterns that can be commercialized.

Three Principal Missions

As a result of these assets, life-styled marketing is coming to play a major part in the three principal innovative missions which most new product developers are called upon to perform on a continuing basis:

1. To bail out an existing product which is selling well below its forecast potential, or whose life cycle is on the down side with sales steadily in decline. In either event, the developer must reposition it to make it at least marginally renewed, if not entirely new.
2. To bring in new profits, requiring the developer to create a range of related new product opportunities for sale in an existing or similar market.
3. To broaden the corporate business base for any one of several reasons, ranging from competitive dominance to legislative regulation to seasonal or cyclical fluctuations in demand. In this case, the developer is usually asked to generate new product opportunities in vaguely defined areas of general interest with many apparent possibilities.

What Life-Styling Is Not

To round out an understanding of the life-styled approach to marketing, it is just as important to know what life styling is not as what it is. The term "life-style," which has a sociological background, was not originally created for application to marketing. When it is used in a commercial sense, therefore, it must not be confused with social trends. Nor, if marketing according to its methods is to have any durability, should it be associated with fads. Finally, the reality on which it is based ought to be carefully distinguished from hypothesis and conjecture.

Life-Styling vs. Marketing to Social Trends

Because life-styling is extracted from the vitality of the marketplace, it is concerned with living phenomena of customer groups: the attitudes and activities that coincide around their everyday attempts to solve problems or reward desires by the use of commercially available products and services. These attitudes and activities are, of course, influenced by social trends. But life-styling a market does not mean merely analyzing its social trends. Instead, it means defining the principal, commercializable thought-and-action systems that are practiced often enough and importantly enough by enough people to create a profitable demand base for product or service benefits.

Only if this demand base exists can a new product be said to have a *marketable* life-style target—that is, a target pattern of attitudes and activities which require the heavy use of products and services to meet their needs and which can be supplied at a high level of profit.

Married women homemakers in their role as family money managers can compose a marketable life-style target whose demands come from repeatedly thinking out and acting out a complex, interrelated system of household resource allocation. Social trends such as the rise of women's liberation, consumerism, and careerism may influence the number of homemakers who think out and act out a family money manager's role. These same trends may also affect the level of sophistication with which they play the role, thus making an impact on the elasticity of demand as well as its quality. For the supplier of budget planning services, vacation planning services, or meal planning services, as well as the manufacturer of home copiers, computers, calculators, or adding machines, the life-style role of family money manager is a real, commercializable market.

Similarly, the business executive in his or her life-style roles as problem solver and decision maker can be a qualified commercial prospect for management education courses and materials or subscriptions to trade magazines and newsletters. Social trends such as a rise in the level of introspection or a renewed pursuit of novelty and change may influence the climate within which business managers must solve problems and make decisions. These trends may act to heighten their sensitivity to problem solving or their interest in more innovative decision making, and therefore they may have a determining effect on the characteristics which new products must deliver in order to be acceptable.

But the marketable life-style is not the social trend called the "flight from functionalism" which helps instill a pursuit of novelty. Instead, marketability is found in the ongoing, persistent managerial role of solving problems and making decisions based on market knowledge. Romanticism is a social trend but not a life-style, even though it may modify many life-styled patterns of young people. The same reasoning applies to a social trend toward or away from sentimentality, spiritualism, sensuousness, materialism or antimaterialism, or tolerance for disorder and chaos.

Life-Styling vs. Marketing of Fads

The life-styles which properly concern the new product marketer are rarely fads. For the most part, they are long-term trends in a marketplace, representing attitude and activity patterns which have endured long enough to have become integral to a market or are well on their way to becoming firmly established. Fads are distinguished by extremely short up-and-down life cycles. They are exceedingly difficult to predict far enough in advance to allow for market planning and their survival role is usually too low to permit much *ex post facto* planning. Most fads are initiated by a product, not by a market need. This may be one of the major reasons why they are so transient.

Life-styles, on the other hand, are rooted in market needs. Each life-style comes into being as a patterned response to a system of related needs. In many cases, marketable life-styles have been built up over a number of years. Some of them have become so customary and traditional that, in fact, they practically define the decision maker in the home or in the office. It is virtually impossible to think of the married woman homemaker without recognizing the centrality of her life-style role as family dietitian. Similarly, it is difficult to conceive of the businessman without taking into consideration his life role as learner and applier of problem-solving information.

Because life-style roles are so basic to the purchasers and influencers who determine the success of the product developer's work, they can be researched, modeled, planned for, and marketed to over a sufficient period of time to make a major investment plausible and its payback reasonably predictable. No fad can hold out this promise. Life-style persistence also helps assure the product developer that he will have the time to create and market successive waves of profitable follow-on products to life-styled markets. Not only will the markets be around long enough for him to do this. Because they are constructed around need systems themselves, they can be sold a wide range of product and service systems which deliver interlocking benefits for their needs.

There is an additional advantage that comes to the product developer from the fact that life-styled markets have durability: Since they are held together by their related needs, they can become foundations for total businesses as well as buying segments for new products. Thus a publisher can build a multiproduct and multiservice business to serve the needs of businessmen in their life-style roles as decision makers and problem solvers; a food processor can build a business to serve the needs of homemakers in their life-style roles as family dietians; and a personal products manufacturer can build an interrelated complex of businesses to serve the needs of homemakers in their life-style roles as family physicians. In each case, the corporate objective would be to preempt as much acceptance as possible within its chosen life-styled market by becoming, in effect, *the* family physician company or *the* decision maker's information company.

Life-Styling vs. Assumptive Marketing

Much, if not most, marketing is based on assumptions which are not borne out in the real world. Part of the reason for this is that many product developers are mistaken about where the real world is. It is convenient to think of the corporate world as the real world for two reasons. First of all, it is there and the new product developer is inside it. Second, the corporate world is a world of products. Because they are tangible, they are obviously real. They accumulate in the form of real inventories which generate real costs and occupy real warehousing space, and they are spoken of in a realistic sense as moving bodily through sales into receivables. Conversely, the market is far less tangible. It is outside, comparatively unknown, and often forbiddingly unknowable. Its seemingly fanciful wants, fickle desires, and fleeting needs are viewed as conducive only to loose prediction, never to certainty. Yet it is the market that is indeed the real world.

New product developers invite unacceptably high risks if they base their plans on assumptions rather than on realities about their markets. The greatest of these assumptions is what the market must be like and what, therefore, it should need. Life-styled marketing makes it difficult to work this way. The reason is inherent in the life-styling process itself: It is based on demonstrable thoughts and acts that can be proved to exist in the marketplace. It qualifies this reality and can enable it to be quantified also. Life-styling therefore confronts the developer with the constant reminder that it is the company, not the market, that is an assumptive world. It forces the developer to consider new products as assumptions based on the calculated risk that they will be acceptable to market life-styles, let alone preferable to them. And furthermore, the developer is put on constant notice that new product concepts are not deserving of the name "products" until they have received market acceptance and that the benefits which he has perceived for them must be regarded as alleged benefits until they have been validated in the real world of his marketplace.

A product whose benefits are alleged by its developer but denied or derided by its market is, in all honesty, simply *scrap*—high-priced scrap, finely tooled scrap, perhaps extremely innovative scrap, but scrap nonetheless. One of the chief functions of life-styled marketing is to reduce the proportion of scrap to new products by reducing the developer's proportion of assumptions to his real-world orientation.

The attitude and activity patterns on which marketable life-styles can be conceived are for the most part openly perceptible in the real world. Certainly a market's activities are overt; by definition they must be. For life-styling purposes, they are most usefully categorized as discretionary and nondiscretionary. Overt attitudes are expressed directly either in action or as accompaniments to action. Other attitudes, including some which can predispose in favor of or against purchase, are covert. Fortunately, a large number of covert attitudes, such as religious and political attitudes, are not commercializable, and therefore need not concern the developer. However, other covert personal attitudes are of particular interest to the new product developer, and, to ferret them out, he must turn to the tools of marketing research. These distinctions among real-world attitudes and activities are illustrated in Exhibit 1.

Criteria for Determining Marketability
of Life-Styles

The central question confronting the new product developer who wants to use a life-styled marketing approach can be simply stated this way: *What life-styles are my potential markets?* Developers and marketers of new products will find six criteria useful in helping them qualify the most suitable life-styles for their own purposes.

1. *Must exist in the real world.* A life-style that is a potential market is a living, ongoing pattern of attitudes and activities. It exists today and therefore is currently observable. It may have existed yesterday, although it need not have existed many years ago. It can predictably be ex-

Exhibit 1. Real-world attitudes and activities which underlie life-styled markets.

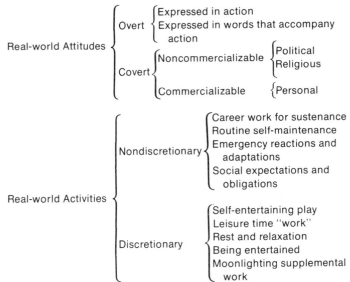

pected to continue to exist tomorrow and for enough tomorrows to accommodate a minimal product or service life cycle of three to five years.

2. *Must be reasonably discrete.* The life-style must be a recognizable entity and hang together as a related whole. A good rule of thumb is that it must be homogeneous within and heterogeneous between. That is, its component roles must be closely interrelated, yet it should be perceptibly different in kind and degree from all other life-styles. Some amount of overlap between life-styles is probably inevitable, but it should be small. This still allows a life-style to meet the test of being reasonably discrete as an organic whole.

3. *Must be commercializable.* Any life-style that is a potential market requires commercial products and services to satisfy the needs which are created by its attitude and

activity patterns. Furthermore, it requires the heavy use of such products and services, thereby guaranteeing that it will offer a major marketing opportunity to the developer. A life-style's needs must demand commercial products and services for their satisfaction, and require them in volume. Otherwise, the life-style cannot be considered a potential market.

4. *Must be "meaningfully repetitive."* The life-style must be important to its participants, occupying enough of their personal or professional lives and accounting for sufficiently serious aspects of life to be perceived by them as meaningful. By its repetitive nature, it reasserts its meaningfulness periodically and therefore motivates successive product or service use and re-use. This in turn helps underwrite the heavy consumption turnover rates which most new product developers and marketers look for.

5. *Must be quantifiable.* The life-style's practitioners must be quantifiable in terms of what developers call the numbers (or "the nums," for short). The principal numbers include the total population of the life-style and its component roles, the percentage of heavy users, their vital statistics such as gross dollars spent on satisfying the needs of the life-style and the sum of still-unspent discretionary income available for further investment, and their traditional demographic figures.

6. *Must be susceptible to advertising.* A life-style must have a sufficient harmony of needs and be responsive to enough similarity of benefits so that a common advertising approach can be directed to it. This means that it must accept the same advertising appeals, the same rank order of benefits, and the same media of advertising distribution. New products which are designed from their inception to fit a life-styled market's needs are in effect being tailored for their eventual advertising appeal to life-styled use situations in the real world.

Deriving Life-Style Roles

The act of seizing a market's concept by life-styling its most significant attitude and activity patterns derives its substance from three types of input: One is observational; the second is informational; and the third is subjective, relying on the new product developer's individual creativity.

The product developer's ability to observe the thought-and-action patterns of his intended market is the single most important aspect of life-styling. In most cases, the life-styles to which he will gear his development already exist in his marketplace. Only rarely will he be "trending"—that is, trying to perceive trends in life-styles before they become easily observational. This is certainly true for repositioning assignments. A repositioned product must generally find its acceptance within existing market patterns. This puts a premium on the developer's capacity for keying in on what his market is thinking and doing, and why.

Look-ins and Live-ins

To build up his capacity, the developer will find it helpful to conduct many look-ins on his market's life-style roles. He will want to watch them in action in the field, over-hear them, and observe the representations of themselves which they accept in their most heavily consumed media. In addition to look-ins, he may need to participate in live-ins with them so he can experience for himself the substance as well as the form of the life-styles he must serve. By living the life-style roles of his markets as much as possible, the developer can test the market for the differences between how they really live out their life-styles and how he may assume they do. This is the only way that the life-styled market orientation of the new product developer can be made realistic.

As a supplement to his observational perceptions of market life-styles, the developer will usually require a validation of his findings by means of market research. Formal research surveys can accomplish two objectives. Quantitatively, they can help him bear out his observations by broadening the size of the sample so that his life-styling is more readily projectable to a national market. They can also help him in a qualitative manner by complementing his personal insights with documentary data on demographic characteristics and psychographic expressions of market needs. Through research, he can also expose some rough-cut product or service concepts as a screening device whose acceptance or rejection will further help him to define his market's life-styles.

Eternal Verities and Current Realities

As the developer looks in and lives in with his markets, we have seen that he will find many of the life-styles he detects to be eternal verities. They have been constant and pervasive for years, and presumably they will endure. The eternal verities are marginally changeable, however, even as they endure; current realities alter them and their needs. For example, as the importance of breakfast has diminished in the average family, the homemaker's role as family dietitian has undergone change. The role itself endures, but its needs and the benefits they demand are not the same. This is an illustration of how social change can introduce current realities which modify life-styles. (Other illustrations of this—the changing role of women in today's society and the new marketing strategies that will be necessary to profit from these trends—are discussed in Chapter 4.) Technological changes are also capable of being important modifiers. The advent of functional foods which deliver health benefits along with good taste and nutrition is blending certain aspects of two prime homemaker life-styles: family dietitian and family physician. Once again, each style endures but it has a new and importantly different profile.

The Naming Process

If his observations and his research conclusions reinforce each other, the developer's remaining task in deriving the life-style roles he will work with is to classify them. This is largely a subjective process. Every developer will approach it somewhat differently, depending on his own type and level of creativity and the specific product area of his concern. The end result of a classification system for life-style roles is its nomenclature. The colloquial, shorthand terminology by which a life-style will be known plays a very important part in the life-styled marketing approach. Each developer should be comfortable with his system. It must be clear to him, for example, that "family physician" is the best term for defining the paraprofessional patterns of attitudes and activities practiced by women homemakers in relation to their families' health. If it is not, he should not use the term but should create instead another name whose meaning is clearer to him and more instantly revealing of the pattern it summarizes. The same injunction holds true for the names of the specific roles within each general life-style.

For life-styled classifications of commercializable patterns practiced by homemakers, the developer's concept of his market will be helped significantly if he is able to express them in *managerial terms*—that is, defining the homemaker as manager or director of an important thought-and-action process. First of all, this gives the developer an accurate insight into what the homemaker really does. Second, it provides him with a way of grasping the framework of her concern in running each key area of her life. His job will be to attach new products to that framework so they will seem natural and necessary in their context.

For businessmen, the developer will find it automatic to style them according to managerial classes since the practice of role management is what being a businessman is all about. As a matter of fact, the life-styling process serves as a reminder that the homemaker and the businessman have a great deal in common as far as their living modes are concerned: Both have jobs or, more professionally expressed, careers. Both types of career make it imperative for them to be efficient, economical organizers of need patterns. Both generally require combinations of product and service systems to satisfy their needs. The systems that both work with are often complex, are usually expensive, and demand many similar purchase decisions. And both the homemaker and the businessman carry an ultimate responsibility in their own spheres which they accept seriously and from which there is little appeal in the event of catastrophic failure.

When the developer puts his observed and researched awareness into the creation of nomenclature, he will be formulating his own life-styling system. This will be the framework within which his planning and testing will take place. For this reason, it must make sense to him. For this reason also, it can very rarely be imposed on him from above or from without. What this says it that life-styling emphasizes the developer's individuality for uniquely conceiving basic, even universally shared, factual data. It thereby gives him and his company the chance to come up with truly different solutions even to common marketing problems that his company may share with several close competitors.

The Role of Life-Styling in New Product Development

Life-styling is the first step in a new product development process that wants to meet the primary real-world needs of its markets with a broad range of options. Once the developer's markets have been life-styled, he can generate the information he requires about the needs revealed in their attitude and activity patterns, and can create, test, and validate new product concepts to meet these needs. He can then prepare for marketing with a systematic life-styled product and promotional approach.

In Exhibit 2, the new product development process has been segmented into four sequential stages. Life-styled market identification takes place in the first stage. The marketing of life-styled products and their promotion through life-styled advertising and sales strategies take place in the last stage. In between these two life-styled "bookends," the new product developer's experimentation processes occur. A brief summary of these four stages will help clarify the process.

Life-Styling Development

In this stage, a market is identified for the first time in a life-styled manner according to the chief attitude and activity patterns that it thinks out and acts out. Each pattern is described as finitely as possible in the form of a scenario which centers on three components: who the life-stylist is in a demographic and psychographic sense; what the life-

Exhibit 2.   The role of life-styling in the new product development process.

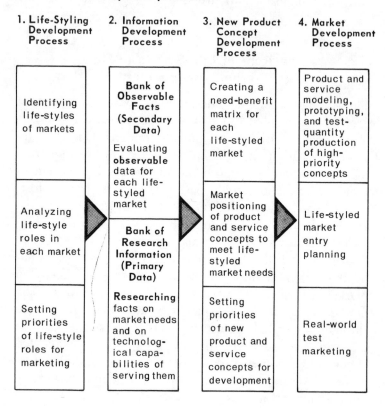

1. Life-Styling Development Process	2. Information Development Process	3. New Product Concept Development Process	4. Market Development Process
Identifying life-styles of markets	**Bank of Observable Facts (Secondary Data)** Evaluating observable data for each life-styled market	Creating a need-benefit matrix for each life-styled market	Product and service modeling, prototyping, and test-quantity production of high-priority concepts
Analyzing life-style roles in each market	**Bank of Research Information (Primary Data)**	Market positioning of product and service concepts to meet life-styled market needs	Life-styled market entry planning
Setting priorities of life-style roles for marketing	Researching facts on market needs and on technological capabilities of serving them	Setting priorities of new product and service concepts for development	Real-world test marketing

style consists of in terms of attitudes and activities; and what commercial opportunities can be generated for new products and services which can newly fill its need gaps or can supplement, complement, or replace existing purchases. Here is an extract from a scenario on the family physician life-style role, showing how some of its attitude and activity patterns can be described and the way in which commercial opportunities may be integrated with them:

The mass, middle majority married woman homemaker in her life-style role as a family physician is essentially concerned with the feeling, the appearance, and the substance of her family's health—she wants them to feel healthy, look healthy, and be healthy. Her primary role is health maintenance. In this aspect of her role, she thinks and acts very much like an insurance agent for her family. Her concerns are principally *preventive*. The second aspect of her role is acutely critical, generally overtaking her with little or no warning. This is the emergency *therapeutic* aspect of family health care. Insofar as possible, she places her reliance on routine maintenance to ward off emergencies. When they happen despite her best efforts, she needs to feel prepared with appropriate products and information services as adequately as possible.

The attitude and activity pattern of family physician is extremely sober and serious. Health is never a laughing matter. The woman homemaker is therefore best addressed when she is in this role as a rational, caring, protective, and businesslike person who carries a severe responsibility. Accordingly, products and information services designed to serve her must be exemplary in their dependability, reliability, and guaranteed performance.

When a life-style has been identified as a thought-and-action system that has a strong sense of unity, when it repeats itself frequently, is important, and initiates needs for the heavy use of products and services, this general definition must be divided into its principal parts called *life-style roles*. They are the net result of life-styled market identification. As such, they serve as the genuine target areas for new product development, since the larger life-styles they make up are simply too vast and encompassing for marketing. The final step in this stage of the developmental process is to assign a priority to each life-style role. This will rank its development time on the basis of its apparent potential and its consonance with existing corporate capabilities.

Information Development

Once a group of life-styled market roles has been assigned priorities, the developer will have to learn as many facts as possible about the practitioners of each high-priority role. Usually he will first compile a data bank of observable facts, which will be composed of secondary information. Most of the material already exists in one form or another or is discoverable by observation. Sometimes this will take him a long way toward his goal of learning what each role's target group does and does not do, how it does it, what products and services currently fit these patterns, what products and service possibilities are currently missing from these patterns or are unsatisfactory, what attitudes are expressed along with these activity patterns, and, equally important, what attitudes remain repressed and have not yet found a commercial outlet.

As need areas emerge from this process of reality sifting, the developer will also have to accumulate a parallel data bank on existing technical capabilities to meet these needs. His own corporate capabilities are his logical first source; research into other technical sources and into the outputs of technological forecasting will generally follow. This will initiate the developer's second data bank, whose information is discoverable only through investment in primary research. It will extend into the market research area, too, as the developer learns what more he needs to know than his secondary data bank can tell him. When market research is used in this way, the contribution it makes to the new product development process can be determined according to its incremental value as an information source.

New Product Concept Development

Given the need patterns observed and researched in a life-styled market, a matrix can be created which will relate each need pattern to benefits that can satisfy or solve it. Benefits are causes of satisfaction; products are the vehicles that deliver benefits. Working from the need–benefit matrix, the new product developer will be able to derive a range of product concepts which have an inferred potential for delivering acceptable benefits for a life-style role. He can then subject these concepts to testing, advertising positioning, and priority positioning in terms of the preference pull they generate in market validation.

This third stage of the new product development process is the most creative phase. It is the first payoff stage for life-styled marketing approaches, since it is here that new product ideas and their promotional presentation themes are born. If life-styling has been successfully employed as a method of seizing the concept of a market, the resulting product and promotional concepts that emerge from this stage of the process should be rich in market value. They should also be highly meaningful to their markets and readily perceived as filling a unique need and performing a significantly valuable new service.

Market Development

The last stage of the new product development process is developing a market. It generally consists of making a working model prototype of a product or service concept, running it in small quantities, planning the life-styling of its market entry so that it can become readily identifiable to its market target as being "for us," and then testing it in the real world of the marketplace.

This is the second payoff stage for life-styling and its

acid test. The new product or service should fit in quickly and decisively with the system of attitude and activity patterns for which it has been designed. Furthermore, its advertising, sales promotion, and sales strategies should create high levels of market awareness along with a high degree of positive attitude-building.

Benefits of a Life-Styled Marketing Approach

Life-styled marketing offers new product developers and marketers three major benefits that other approaches rarely deliver—or cannot deliver at all. These benefits may be strung together into a theme for life-styling which can claim for it richer, market-oriented product and service options generated and marketed at reduced risk. Broken out, These individual benefits may be summarized as follows:

1. *Richer new product options.* Life-styling can inundate the developer's mind with a broad range of options for new products. Since every life-styled market he explores is a *system* of interrelated attitudes and activities, the need-seeking information he gets back will itself be in the form of systems. When contrasted with the discovery of single needs as a result of using other methods, need systems can often stimulate the developer's capacity for response by supplying him with an unexpected richness of inputs. Quantitatively, there is likely to be a great amount of material. Qualitatively, in most cases it will tend to be highly charged with provocative, challenging information seeded thickly with product opportunity. It is not unusual for one rather moderate market research sweep of a life-styled market to yield a great deal more information than can be dealt with by a single developmental mission.

2. *Built-in market orientation.* New products and ser-

vices which are derived from life-styling are born with market orientation. Having sprung conceptually from the very need systems to which they will return commercially through marketing, they should have true customer relevance as problem-solving solutions to life-style patterns. In this way, the market orientation that so many new products lack is built into products which are life-styled. It is also built into their advertising. In theory, advertising achieves its greatest cost-effectiveness when it can position its products in a real-world situation with which its users can strongly identify. When a new product is life-styled from its inception, its advertising theme and positioning are also inherently part of it as it is prepared for market entry. These same benefit systems can easily be reflected back to their originators in the life-styled market where they were first uncovered, and thus they can appeal to a particular use situation which is, in a sense, waiting for them.

3. *Reduced risk.* It is less hazardous to market a life-styled product benefit system to a life-styled market need system than to attempt to market a single product benefit to a single market need. In the first instance, the developer has the odds going for him: Even if his system of product benefits does not mesh on a one-for-one basis with the market's total need system, enough of the key benefit propositions may achieve acceptance to reduce the risk of failure. Thus, a security factor of significant proportions exists on this system-to-system basis.

Without it, the developer may have to put all his eggs in one basket—that is, he may have to try to market to a single assumed market need. If he misjudges too much of the precise nature of this solitary need, he invites disaster, because he has no margin. Life-styling grants him a comparatively broad margin because he is targeting at least a couple of interrelated needs and can be successful even if fewer than all of them are satisfied by his new product or service system.

In the following three chapters of this book, these benefits will be highlighted by the study of the life-styled marketing method in action in genuine new product development problems. Each of the problems is a tough one, all too likely to occur regularly over the short-term life cycle of any consumer or industrial manufacturer or service organization. First, a new product developer will be shown using the strategies of life-styled marketing to create new product opportunities in existing products. Then a product developer will be shown creating a range of related new opportunities for sale in his present market and similar markets by the use of life-styling techniques. And finally, a developer will be shown generating product opportunities in a new area of general interest to his company but which his management has only vaguely defined for him.

2

Life-Styling to Create New Product Opportunities in Existing Products

Products pursue markets, sometimes faultily but always as a reaction to market needs. Markets, however, are on the move. Their needs change or the priorities change with which their needs are held. Postponable needs become urgent and apparently enduring needs turn out to be short-term fads. New problems claim a market's attention, or new solutions are needed for old problems. As a result, a product may lose its fit, because it no longer matches up with its market's perception of the optimal benefit—or perhaps even of an acceptable one.

Life-styling offers many products a second chance to position themselves. A product may have been originally positioned without life-styling. Now it can be. Or, less frequently, it may have been positioned for the wrong life-style. Now it can be corrected.

Product planners and market analysts do not have to be badly wrong to be seriously off target in selecting a product's single most crucial benefit. A slight deviation from a market's core need can account for a sizable loss of profit.

This is why there is such a premium on the ability to "come down Main Street"—that is, pinpoint a need exactly.

The converse of this truism enables a product to take on a second life, to be born again. If a slight deviation in market targeting can exact a sizable profit penalty, a slight repositioning can often revoke the penalty and return a sizable reward.

Repositioning that takes place in "real life" and in full view of consumers, customers, and competitors is never easy. "Macy's window" is not the best place for making a marketing turnaround, yet it is frequently necessary. Life-styling helps make it possible and can go a long way to ensuring its success.

Several case histories will illustrate this proposition. The first case will treat at length the repositioning of a beer according to life-styled strategies. This case will be followed by a selection of "minicases" of a broad range of products and services that have been successfully repositioned to meet the attitude and activity patterns of a life-style. In each case, the original unsuccessful positioning will be given, along with the product's chief benefits. Then the life-styled repositioning will be summarized. (The life-styles referred to are identified in detail in Appendix A.)

The conceptual thinking behind these life-styled approaches has followed the first five phases of the product repositioning plan shown in its entirely in Exhibit 3. The products and services that have undergone repositioning have been selected to illustrate life-styled renovation for two reasons. First of all, they are universally known products, so that understanding their conversion requires no exotic technological knowledge. Second, they reveal the two most common reasons for repositioning: they suffer from sameness or they are off target.

Exhibit 3. Life-styled product repositioning plan.

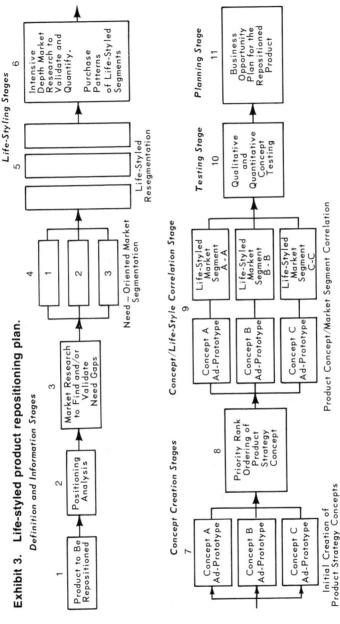

The case histories point up the value of life-styling in guiding developers and marketers to conceive of their products in ways that make a tight market fit with their customers—that is, to come as close as possible to a one-to-one relationship between their product benefits and market needs. Sometimes a life-styled repositioning is astonishingly simple: A market is life-styled according to its principal attitude and activity patterns, and presto! a product position jumps out. At other times an exceedingly complex analysis must be undertaken. This is generally required where traditional products are concerned, especially if they have been marketed by traditional features-and-benefits approaches that are frozen by custom and encrusted with habit.

The three progressive matrix diagrams that comprise Exhibit 4 show some of the stress and strain that went into squeezing out product repositioning concepts for a simple product like traditional potato chips. For each life-styled role that was conceived in the snack market where potato chips are sold, the major question asked was this: What product and promotional benefits for the married women homemakers who are playing this role will have the greatest chance of preempting the established competition?

Exhibit 4a: Life-style/product strategy concept inventory. The first matrix represents the developer's total conceptual inventory of six market life-styles and several of the product strategy concepts which have occurred to him as potentially matching their needs. The life-styles are arranged vertically from A to F down the left-hand side of the matrix. To maintain a proper proportional representation with consumer influences in the snack food market, four life-style roles have been assigned to women, and one each for men and children.

As it stands, the matrix in Exhibit 4a is unworkable. It is nonetheless the necessary first step in the developer's

Exhibit 4a. Life-style/product strategy concept inventory.

MARKET LIFE-STYLE	PRODUCT STRATEGY CONCEPTS	
A	Children in their life-style role as "random demanders"	1. Children's fun chips	Crunchy, textured, multishaped and multisized, taste surprises, fun image
		2. Children's flavor chips	Taste surprises, taste varieties, good tasting, diet supplement, Ovaltine image
		3. Health chips	Vitamin chips, mineral chips, milk image of basic food
B	Women in their life-style role as family dietitians	1. Health chips	Vitamin chips, mineral chips, milk image of basic food
		2. Family fun chips	Picnic and cookout chips, wholesome family image
		3. Children's fun chips	Crunchy, textured, multishaped and multisized, taste surprises, fun image, treat chips for reward
C	Women in their life-style role as good hostesses	1. Flavor chips	Eat by themselves or as dip chips, hostess-approval image of group acceptance
		2. Unusual chips	Ultrasophisticated, high-style chips, unique tastes and ingredients, Miller Hi-Life image of creative homemaking and status conferral
D	Women in their life-style role as family physicians	1. Cosmetic chips	Diet chips to be eaten with or in place of meals, to take edge off appetite, Sego image of low-calorie food
		2. Health chips	Vitamin chips, mineral chips, milk image of basic high-protein food, fresh and wholesome, pure, nourishing, nongreasy to connote low fat
E	Women in their life-style role as liberated jetsetters	1. Health chips	Vitamin chips, mineral chips, milk image of basic food, also cosmetic diet concerns
		2. Aphrodisiac chips	Energy chips, seductive personal magnetism effect, libidinous image
F	Men in their life-style role as swingers	1. Health chips	Vitamin chips, mineral chips, milk image of basic food
		2. Aphrodisiac chips	Energy chips, seductive personal magnetism effect, libidinous image, nongreasy to permit hand holding

repositioning method because it releases his stored-up universe of possibilities and probabilities, both of markets and of product concept strategies. It is essential for him to get them out of his head and put them down on paper in some sort of structural format. This allows him to see what, if anything, he may have to work with. In addition, freeing his backlog of existing ideas allows him to generate new thinking in its place without merely repeating familiar concepts.

Each life-style role in Exhibit 4a has been given a code letter designation. These code letters can be paired with the code numbers assigned to each product strategy concept as a means of shorthand identification for a life-style/product concept match-up. Thus the designation D1 identifies the cosmetic chips concepts as a new product strategy relating to market life-style D for women in their role as family physicians.

Along with their physician role, three other life roles for women are listed in the matrix: as caring and provident family dietitians, as attentive hostesses, and as vigorous jet-setters. Two other life-styles are also listed. One is for men in their role of vigorous, masculine swingers. The other is for children as random demanders.

In the first matrix stage of concept development, it is safest to regard the concept inventory which appears opposite each life-style category as being composed of underlying *strategies* for concepts rather than concepts themselves. This approach should encourage the developer to generate the broadest spectrum of product possibilities which are constrained only by their gross potential for commercialization. In the second matrix, most of these strategy ideas will be culled. The surviving ideas can then be thought of as product concepts. A few of these concepts may then go on to become products.

Following this broad spectrum approach to creating a

concept inventory, eight individual strategy concepts have been generated for product repositioning. Some are repeated for more than one life-style. Of these eight strategies, four will survive into the second matrix and three into the final matrix. This is a typical attrition rate for consumer product categories, where one surviving concept out of every three to five is a respectable average.

Exhibit 4b: Life-style/product concept selection. The matrix in Exhibit 4b is the most crucial stage in the repositioning process. It is the selection stage, where the life-styles and product concepts that will be worked with are determined. This stage is important for what is discarded as well as for what is kept, for only the life-style roles which endure after reduction can go on to become eventually profitable markets. The developer must be careful not to throw the baby out with the bath water. This constraint accounts for the critical role played by this second match-up phase and for its major contribution to repositioning success or failure.

In Exhibit 4b, the developer has begun to make his selections by reducing by three the number of life-style roles he wants to work with. The number of product concepts has also been reduced. In this second stage of his matrix construction, he has made a momentous decision: He has eliminated the good hostess life-style role as a target market. The implications of this decision range far beyond the simple removal of one life-style as a potential market. Since the good hostess role was the originally intended market for the product (although, of course, it was not conceived of in this life-styled term), its abandonment for repositioning will now make it mandatory for the developer to become truly innovative. The most overmarketed area of the snack food field, dominated by well-entrenched leaders, is now going to be left to them.

This decision permits the developer to explore the mar-

Exhibit 4b. Life-style/product concept selection.

MARKET LIFE-STYLE	PRODUCT CONCEPTS	
B Women as family dietitians	B1. Health chips *(Medicine chips)*	(Fits Market Life-Style B) Vitamin chips, mineral chips, milk image of basic high-protein food, the Wheaties of chips; for purchase by children alone, or by exerting influence on mother, or by mother
D Women as family physicians	D1. Cosmetic chips *(Diet chips)*	(Fits Market Life-Style D) Meals complement or replacement—for example, "Slimchips" with Sego image
E Women as jetsetters	E1. Health chips *(Medicine chips)*	(Fits Market Life-Styles B, D, and E) Vitamin chips, mineral chips, milk or Gatorade image of basic energy
	E2. Aphrodisiac chips *(Sex chips)*	(Fits Market Life-Style E) Libidinous energy chips; a his-and-her chip sized and shaped for romantic, seductive settings

Exhibit 4c. Life-style/product concept match-up.

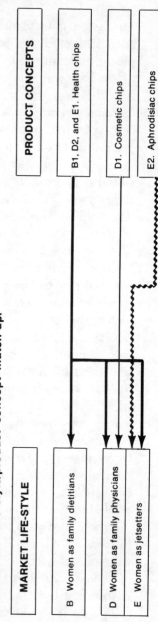

MARKET LIFE-STYLE
B Women as family dietitians
D Women as family physicians
E Women as jetsetters

PRODUCT CONCEPTS

B1, D2, and E1. Health chips

D1. Cosmetic chips

E2. Aphrodisiac chips

ried woman homemaker's other life roles to see if he can bring genuine new benefits to any of them in snack food form. Is there a formulation, or promotional platform, that can add perceived value to the living patterns of the family dietitian, the family physician, or the jetsetter? To find an answer to this question, the developer will have to measure his surviving product concepts against his three remaining life-styles and see if he can make contact anywhere among them.

Whenever a life-styled market fails to survive the selection process, it becomes essential for the developer to try to relate each concept of his matrix to more than one of the remaining life-styles. This is a vital strategy because life-style roles are precious. For any marketer, there are always comparatively few life-styles that are potential markets as opposed to the number of product concepts which can be created for their acceptance. By dropping a life-style role such as the good hostess, the developer has given away a major category of product use. He has also made an executive decision not to draw on the information base he possesses—and has earned at great cost for his company—about the good hostess market. In other words, he is deliberately allowing a corporate knowledge resource to become unemployed. Not only will this investment be unable to pay back many dividends in the repositioning process, but the developer may now have to incur new costs in establishing an initial knowledge base for one or more of his remaining life-styled markets.

For these reasons, every life-styled market and every product concept that can be related to it should be exploited as intensively as possible. In his manipulation of the matrix in Exhibit 4*b*, the developer has followed this policy. In addition, one of his concepts, health chips, has been related to three market life-styles: the family dietitian, family physician, and jetsetter.

Exhibit 4c: Life-style/product concept match-up. The third matrix in Exhibit 4 illustrates the developer's final match-up of life-styles and concepts for a newly positioned product. Three product concept possibilities have emerged:

1. An *aphrodisiac chip*, a libidinous energy chip for consumption on romantic husband–wife occasions by the young married woman homemaker in her life-style role as jetsetter.

2. A *cosmetic chip*, a low-calorie mealtime complement or replacement chip for the diet-control use of the married woman homemaker in her life-style role as family physician. In arriving at this concept, the developer has reinvented the basic idea which already has found product application in the Metrecal wafer.

3. A *health chip* containing nutritive vitamins, minerals, protein, and other basic food values for purchase and use by the married woman homemaker in any one of three life-style roles: family dietitian, family physician, and jetsetter. This concept contains some of the values of high-protein dry cereals which are sometimes eaten as snacks, but it goes considerably beyond cereals in the full range of its implications.

As he begins to elaborate on the match-ups he has created, the developer can see that he has put together a challenging trio of conceptual repositionings. One concept, that of aphrodisiac chips, is a totally new product idea aimed at a life-style to which snack foods are rarely, if ever, directly marketed. Cosmetic chips, the second concept, is somewhat competitive with similar products that are already on the market and that promise diet control benefits. Their positions, however, are not universally pinpointed for the family physician life-style. The third concept is for health and nutrition chips, a master concept that can be customized for any of the three life-style roles the developer has earmarked for study. This is another totally new concept with no close market correlates.

A box score of these options summarizes the range of new opportunities which have settled out of the developer's market styling. Two totally new concepts have been created in the form of aphrodisiac chips and health chips. One reasonably familiar concept has been reiterated by cosmetic chips, coupled in one case to a life-style role that has at best some historical preparation for accepting snack foods as a vehicle for diet control benefits.

The Repositioning of Blue Max Beer

Blue Max Beer was developed for its original market entry to appeal to the higher-priced end of the regular beer market, which contains one out of every four beer drinkers. About 40 percent of all beer volume is concentrated here. So are the heavy users. Six out of every ten drinkers in this market segment consume a minimum of ten 12-ounce glasses of beer every week—almost 15 times the national average. These heavy users must therefore be the key market target for any regular beer.

Original Approaches to Positioning

Market Concentration Factors

Blue Max's developers began their work by facing the central fact that the beer market is a male market. More than two-thirds of all regular beer drinkers are men. Among them, they account for more than 80 percent of all beer volume. Half of this volume is consumed by men between the ages of 21 and 40, most of whom are middle-income earners. Throughout many generations of marketing, these key facts have formed the core of the brewing industry's approach to product development, sales, and advertising. For old and new beers alike, "where the men are" has almost invariably been at the middle-income, middle-education, and low- to middle-age ranges.

Beer is a refreshment product. A brewer is therefore in the refreshment business. Because of the age-old mythology of brewing and the fact that beer is an alcoholic refreshment, beer serves refreshment needs that are different in type and degree from other needs for other products such as soft drinks, cigarettes, and chewing gum. Beer is unique in that it allows people to suspend their inhibitions, get together with other people, and escape from their traditional "selves."

Most beer developers have assumed that there are two principal types of men in their market and that they can best be defined in attitudinal terms. One is the *affiliator*, the man who has a high need to affiliate with others and who prefers beer as a symbol of companionship, fellowship, and what some psychologists call a lubricant for group dynamics. For this type of man, getting together over a beer is an act of social refreshment as well as physiological renewal. The second major type of man in the beer market can be regarded as the *escapist*, the man who seeks the rewards of fantasy that enable him to act out or imagine exploits that his daily life routines deny him. Men who need an escapist opportunity through beer, or perhaps because they cannot afford or gain access to alternative methods of getting away, take on the roles of mythical adventurers, athletes, heroes, and other overtly masculine figures in their self-perceptions. The strong association between beer and sports is at least somewhat explained by this fact.

It is a useful fiction for the developer to try to model

these concepts. Accordingly, each of the two major types of beer consumer has been positioned along an axis in Exhibit 5*a*. Axis A-B is the *affiliation axis*. The high affiliators—beer drinkers with a higher-than-average need for the benefits of affiliation—cluster at the A terminal. Another axis runs along line C-B. This is the *escapist axis*. Here again, the high escapists tend to cluster at one terminal (this time it is at C). At the points where the high affiliators and the high escapists cluster, the two axes are farthest from each other. Eventually, however, they merge at point B. This is where the combined affiliators

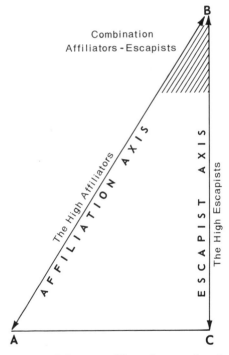

Exhibit 5a. **Beer drinkers positioned according to needs for affiliation and escape.**

and escapists are found. When line A-C is drawn, a triangle is formed. Most beer sales occur within its boundaries. This will be seen when Exhibit 5*b* is compared with Exhibit 5*a*.

Product Concentration Factors

Where the men are—or, in any event, where they have been seen to be by brewers—has historically determined where most beers are positioned. This is natural. By definition, any market-oriented business must center on the needs of its heaviest customers. One of the results of this concentration of the beer business around the two basic needs of its heaviest consumers is that the established brands leave few apparent need gaps for newcomer brands to fill. This makes innovation in the beer market, as in so many other concentrated markets, an extremely difficult and costly task if traditional methods of product positioning are used.

Exhibit 5*b* is a predictable outcome of Exhibit 5*a*. It shows how four of the major beer brands have positioned themselves along the axes of affiliation and escapism. Budweiser, long the No. 1 beer, is positioned astride the high affiliators. It presents itself as every man's beer, a part of Americana that invites all beer drinkers to affiliate with it. Miller enjoys a centrist location on the affiliation axis. It, too, is positioned as a product which attracts a consensus of acceptance. Schaefer, a regional beer, is frankly positioned as an escapist product. It appeals to the heavy beer drinker, the man who is "having more than one," by surrounding him with athletic, hyperactive masculine imagery. Schlitz has made itself attractive to both affiliators and escapists, or to beer drinkers who combine both needs. Its market may be thought of as occurring where the axes of affiliation and escapism merge.

Exhibit 5b. **Beer brands positioned according to benefits of affiliation and escape.**

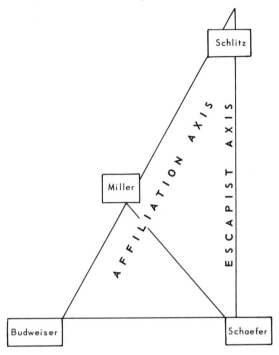

Blue Max Original Marketing Strategy

The Budweiser-Miller-Schlitz-Schaefer triangle is the location for most beer sales (Exhibit 5*b*). As a new beer brand, Blue Max was attracted by the market potential existing within the triangle. Its developer therefore tried to position it originally as a new option for men who wanted a heavily traditional beer. As Exhibit 5*c* shows, he located it along the Schlitz-Miller-Budweiser continuum at point M-1, where it tried to out-Miller Miller. Even though it was a new product, it based its market approach on an old

Exhibit 5c.   Blue Max brand positioned in relation to existing brands.

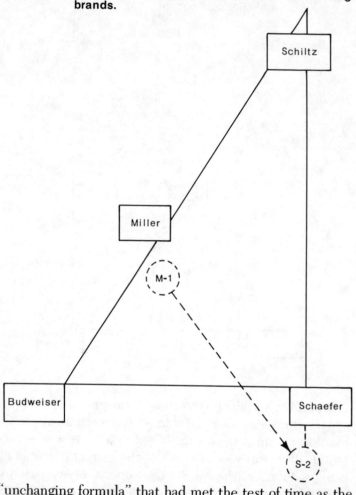

"unchanging formula" that had met the test of time as the "supreme example" of its brewer's skill and geographical advantages for making beer. Its "unique personality" of blending an old formula with a new beer was designed to give Blue Max access to beer drinkers who also possessed "a unique personality" which enabled them to appreciate traditional values as a natural, necessary complement to modern living—as a compensation, in effect, for the very modernity of modern life.

When market share accumulated slowly, the Blue Max developer attempted to shift its position to point S-2, where he wanted to try to out-Schaefer Schaefer. In this new location, it emphasized masculine gregariousness as an active man's beer for men of confidence, nerve, and skillful prowess in high-risk accomplishments. Neither of these attempts to gain a profitable market foothold proved successful. Over a three-year period, Blue Max was unable to sustain an average 2 percent share of the market.

Life-Styled Approaches to Repositioning

At this point in Blue Max's life cycle, it is interesting to analyze the developer's thinking process to see how a life-styled approach to its repositioning can provide marketable new insights. A life-styling of the regular beer market has two objectives for Blue Max: to find productive new ways of seizing the concept of the heavy beer-drinking market that will depart meaningfully from the traditional market discriminators that all other brewers use, and to identify a concept that holds the greatest promise of mobilizing a profitable share of the market (if indeed those ways can be found).

A life-styled approach to repositioning Blue Max will take its developer through three steps. First, the beer drinkers' commercial life cycle must be plotted. This forms the time frame within which the next step takes place, that of creating and assigning life-style roles to Blue Max customers. Then, in the third step, new positioning concepts must be derived for Blue Max from the life-style roles.

Beer Drinkers' Commercial Life Cycle

All life-styles exist within a time frame called a life cycle, a continuous circle that represents the chronological maturing process of an industry's customers from the moment of their commercial "birth" through senescence. For a baby food marketer, the age of commercial birth at which his market (babies) develops important marketable needs is between six and twelve months. The mothers who are the decision makers are usually 20 to 30 years beyond in their own life cycles. Baby food marketers thus concentrate on the first 30 years or so of the life cycle and, of secondary importance, the geriatric market of the life cycle's sixth, seventh, and eighth decades. For a brewer, the principal phases of the commercial life cycle are those that encompass the chief beer consumption years between a man's 20th and 40th birthdays. This age range constitutes the time frame within which the key life-style roles occur that can apply to beer marketing.

Exhibit 6 illustrates a life-cycle time frame which accommodates the 20- to 40-year age range for men. Within it, four phases containing nine discrete life-style roles have been located. Each of these life-style roles has been identified by a combination of two procedures: (1) observation of life-stylists who are living the roles, and the products, advertising, and media which have been successfully designed to reach them; and (2) marketing research of a behavioral, attitudinal nature. Once identified, each role has been given a descriptive name which is useful as a colloquial shorthand for pinpointing its core attitude and activity patterns. In this case, following the method worked out with Pat Gorman, Jim Gouthro, and Paul Pohle (on behalf of the Joseph Schlitz Brewing Company), it was decided by the developer that the more usual management nomenclature for life-styles would be less inspirational for Blue Max repositioning than would

Exhibit 6.   Life-style roles for men within the time frame of the beer drinker's commercial life cycle.

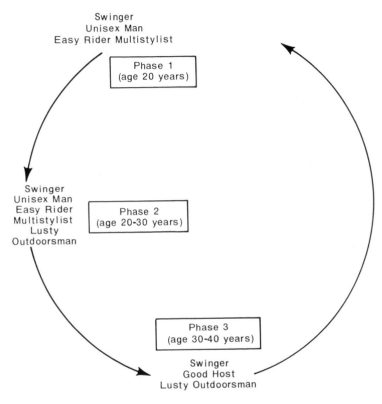

names which reflect the most vital aspects of the beer drinker's affiliation and escapist patterns.

The reason for this exceptional decision reveals some of the adaptability of a life-styling strategy of repositioning. There is a good deal of truth to the argument that the affiliation and escapist attitudes and activities which accompany beer consumption demand some sort of management by the beer drinker. This approach to beer visualizes it as a self-management tool for aiding in affiliation and escape. It has resulted in the traditional "beer belongs" image which most of the well-entrenched brands have popularized. It could equally well result in assigning role-management names to beer drinkers.

Another approach, however, and the one taken here, is to suggest that the life-cycle curve for beer drinking exists as an entity in itself that can be superimposed over the normal, routine management cycle that all responsible men live out. The beer drinker can then be regarded as a man who commutes into the superimposed life cycle of beer drinking to escape periodically from his repetitive, tightly managed, and very responsible life cycle or to seek affiliations that his managerial living cycle denies him.

A natural corollary of this approach is to expect that affiliative and escapist life-style roles will persist throughout a wide range of age groupings. As Exhibit 6 shows, they can. Three of the life-style roles of the 20-year age phase are shown by Exhibit 6 to persist into the second phase of the life cycle which accommodates the 20- to 30-year age range. In turn, two of the roles from that age range overlap into the third phase of the life cycle. This awareness of the persistence of roles and the marketing continuity that it suggests—despite age changes—is one of the advantages of the life-styling approach to beer marketing over a brewer's more usual demographic market classification based largely on transient age dimensions.

Life-Style Roles for Blue Max Consumers

The term "phase 1" is used in Exhibit 6 to pinpoint the moment when the life cycle for men first becomes commercializable for a brewer at a significant volume of business. This occurs at about the 20th year of life. At this time in a young man's life cycle, he is likely to be acting out or fantasizing one of several life-style roles that have relevance to beer consumption. Three of these roles are mentioned in the exhibit: swinger, unisex man, and easy rider multistylist. These three roles can be summarized as follows:

1. The term *swinger* describes a young, middle majority heavy beer drinker in his life-style role as a hypersocial party giver and party goer; heavy dater and "consumer" of young, middle majority women; and frequent, compulsive food and beverage snacker.

The swinger role is an affiliation role. It is highly fashionable at an early time in a young man's life and in many instances is probably forced on him by social custom and expectation. The role is an intense one, requiring that its players work hard at having fun. It is a noisy, busy, and extremely active role whose consumption activities occupy a major portion of the young man's time and discretionary income. Everything is "consumed" with great speed: people are met and discarded, personal relationships are acquired and eliminated, places and events are used up as they pass from being "in" to being "out," and refreshment foods and beverages enjoy a great turnover. Acting out the role of swinger means that a man is in an extremely kinetic stage of his life and that his beer preferences will be a reflection of his psychological and physiological demonstrativeness.

2. The *unisex man* is a young, middle majority heavy beer drinker in his life-style role as a social and often economic companion to women. He has a heightened propensity to share with them a set of common life-styles, artifacts, apparel, and products on a cooperative, interchangeable basis which emphasizes their sameness and either disguises or obliterates their traditional male–female distinctions.

The unisex man, like the swinger, is also an affiliator. His affiliation is with a concept of himself as part of a couple, however, and not with the swinger's generously heterosexual concept of the rugged, solitary male. The unisex man is likely to be far more conservative in his style than either the swinger or the multistyled easy rider. He is also more stable, more dependable as a customer, and usually more susceptible to continued brand loyalties. His romanticism is most likely to be single-person-oriented, in contrast to the multiperson orientation of the swinger and the mutliple-place orientation of the easy rider. Beer serves as one more bond betwęen him and his woman, something to hold in common as a shared pleasure and indicator of their togetherness. Whereas the swinger's beer is "my beer," the unisex man's beer is generally "our beer."

3. The *easy rider multistylist* is also a young, middle majority heavy beer drinker. But he casts himself in a different role, that of a hyperactive tester and experimenter of multiple life-styles. The common denominator of rootlessness may create a need for rooted, "umbilical" brand relationships that offer continuity.

The easy rider multistylist is an escapist role. As a result, the easy rider—so named because his life-style is actually a continuing transition from one life-style role to another—is an elusive marketing target. He generally prefers to travel light, scorning permanent possessions except those that contribute directly to his mobility. In a similar way, he plays down potential involvements with people or affiliations with established institutions.

Yet, like men in all roles, he too requires a few enduring symbols in his life that defy rapid turnover. Certain brands may supply this need if their fundamental appeal is either companionate on the one hand or open-endedly broad and generalized on the other. Easy riders are heavy consumers of products that permit mobility and offer complete consumption with one serving and easy disposability. Their wastage rate can be as high as their use rate.

Beer meets many of the requirements of such a multi-styled life, being unobstructive, portable, relatively stable over time, and refreshing amidst the psychic or physical hurly-burly of being constantly en route.

Although overlapping is easily possible, each of these three roles is essentially an entity in itself. A swinger is not likely to play the role of unisex man very often, and the unisex man is equally unlikely to act out the swinger's role or become an easy rider unless his man–woman affiliation breaks up. The easy rider, however, can play either of the other two roles—or, indeed, almost any transient role—at any time. This is the essential attribute of his multistyled approach to life, traveling back and forth between variously styled roles as he pleases. But despite this unsettled state, this role and the other two can provide the developer with wide-ranging latitude in creating new product concepts to solve the repositioning problem of a beer.

New Life-Styled Positioning Concepts for Blue Max

The process of life-styling the beer-drinking market's heavy consuming core is only a means for the developer; it is not an end in itself. His objective is to use the life-styles as a base from which to generate rich, uniquely marketable product and promotional concepts which will help him reposition his existing product. Some of the new concepts he creates may involve extensive product reformulations. Other concepts may require only promotional changes. To provoke these concepts from his thinking, the developer will have to ask himself a question concerning each life-style role he has defined in his market: What product and promotional benefits are demanded by the men who are fantasizing and acting out this role in order to satisfy their needs most effectively.

Typically, the developer will call forth more potential

answers to this question than will be technically or economically feasible to use. Some of the concepts he generates will be impossible or too expensive to manufacture. Others will be technically feasible but uneconomical. Many will be both technologically sound and economical, but simply unmarketable. But most will seem plausible, be scientifically possible, and arouse visions of high potential. Since few concepts can ever make such an optical illusion materialize in reality, the developer's creative task in concept-building will always have to be tempered with self-control.

In approaching the repositioning problem for Blue Max, the developer was able to create a broad constellation of marketing concepts for beer which could serve the life-style roles he had time-framed along the beer drinker's commercial life cycle. For three of these styles, he has developed the concepts illustrated on the matrix in Exhibit 7. From the inventory of new concepts he is able to create in this manner, he will later select some of them for concept testing and product prototyping. At this stage in his evolutionary process, helpful insights into the developer's train of thought can be gained by following his reasoning in constructing his hypothesis for a super-masculine beer for the swinger life-style role.

The swinger is a paradoxical man. He professes superior masculinity, but he probably feels inferior or at least he has an unusually pronounced need to reassure himself of his manliness. He does this in many ways: his dress; his use of large-size jewelry and massive adornments such as oversize belt buckles; the way he styles his hair, both on his head and on his face; his choice of lotions and aromatics to add an olfactory dimension to his presence and to linger behind as a recollection of his recent presence; his conspicuous possessions, especially motor vehicles of all types; his style and content of speech. The general impression he creates is of bigness in all

Exhibit 7. Life-styled concept generation for beer.

LIFE-STYLE ROLES	PRODUCT REPOSITIONING CONCEPTS	
	Physical Product Characteristics	Promotional Product Benefits
Swinger	Dark color Strong taste Heavy feel in mouth	"Super-masculine beer" theme with frankly heterosexual appeals; correlation of "BM" initials of Blue Max with "Big Man" motif in advertising and packaging
Unisex Man	Light color Light, neutral taste Light feel in mouth	"A beer for the two of you" or a "His-and-Her Beer" theme with emphatic companionate appeals
Easy Rider Multistylist	Dark color Strong taste Heavy feel in mouth	"Hypertraditional beer" to offer a branded umbilical cord as a connection to an unremembered past
	Light color Light but insistent taste Moderate feel in mouth	"Companion beer" to provide symbolic friendship and sense of rootedness in an otherwise lonely existence
	High carbonation Flavored and colored beers 6-ounce minicans	"Transcendent beer" which escapes from the norms of other beers into unexpected and unconventional tastes or promotional themes

its dimensions; large in stature, even though he himself may be small; loud in sound and in flashy color; fast, both in motion and in behavior toward women. The swinger is a young man at a young time in his life or an older man trying to recapture his youth. This fact makes youthful symbols very important, especially in products. In order for the swinging young man to identify strongly with a brand, it must display the central proof of masculine youthfulness: potency. Beer is ideally suited for this type of positioning since it is so very much a man's product to begin with. What would happen, then, if Blue Max were moved up the masculinity scale to become the most masculine of all beers?

A super-masculine Blue Max would say to the swinger: this is your beer. Its color would probably have to be darkened a bit to give it a strong, heavily male look. Its taste would have to be heavied up, too. So would its apparent feel in the mouth. There is a fine line between a beer being heavy and full but not chewy. We'd have to avoid going overboard on that. But this would be a beer whose first look and taste would say it was for men—real men.

Promotionally, we'd have to firm up our package designs and labeling. We'd need strong artwork, bold lettering, and predominantly male colors such as black and red or blue and gold. The Blue Max cross, the medal after which the beer is named, could be bumped up bigger, too. Maybe it can even be embossed to show up more aggressively and to give a rough-textured feel to the can or label. What about the beer's initials, BM? Perhaps we could play them off the Blue Max name into a dual meaning—something like "big man"—and emphasize our new masculinity around that theme.

Through this sort of free association, the developer can draw upon each of his market's life roles for inspiration to stimulate his conceptual thinking. As he free-associates, he tries to think feelingly, letting the life-style's scenario guide him as he senses it, experiences it, or comes to know it from research. The eventual matrix he arrives at becomes his plotting board for assigning new, repositioned concepts for his own further editorial critique and then to market evaluation. His box score on the matrix in Exhibit 7 shows that he was able to define three life-style roles for beer drinkers, two of which have suggested repositioning concepts. One of these concepts, that of a supermasculine beer, is more or less traditional. The second concept, of a "his-and-her" beer, is innovative. For a third life-style role, the developer has generated three concepts which range from the traditional to the innovative.

As an adjunct to the matrix in Exhibit 7, a positioning device called *contact cards* can also be helpful. Two decks of cards are used for this purpose. One deck, colored red, represents the life-style roles with which the developer is working. The other deck, colored blue, will contain the developer's product concepts. By arranging and rearranging them, the developer can create a movable matrix permitting him to test all his concepts for their potential *contact* with a life-style role. In Exhibit 8, two cards are shown in contact with each other: the easy rider multistylist life role and the product concept of a companion beer.

Life-Styled Repositioning of Twelve Products and Services

The Blue Max case illustrates the in-depth analysis of a mispositioned product that can be achieved through the use of life-styling thought processes. Much the same type of analysis has been applied to many other products and services. In each case, three general statements tended to be true:

Exhibit 8. Life-style role and product concept contact cards in a match-up.

EASY RIDER MULTISTYLIST

The young, middle majority heavy beer drinker in his life-style role as a hyperactive tester and experimenter with multiple life-styles whose common denominator of rootlessness may create a need for rooted, "umbilical" brand relationships that offer continuity.

COMPANION BEER

The beer that goes along with multiple life-styles; a "root" beer offering continuity in a life marked by discontinuities; a me-and-my-beer kind of companion beer that is worthy of the description; "A man's best beer is his friend."

1. The original position of each product or service was along traditional lines, emphasizing features and characteristics and their resultant user benefits.

2. Benefits were expressed in terms of value that would be added to the user in superior degree or quality to competitive values.

3. When repositioning was made, a specific market for the product or service was targeted on a life-styled basis— that is, according to a pattern of attitudes and activities that formed a "need base." Benefits were customized to match up with the targeted life-style so that it became clearly the market segment of choice. Advertising theming, sales strategy, and product packaging were all fashioned to zero in on the life-styled customer. In some cases, the nature of the product or service itself underwent a life-styled change.

The original positioning and eventual life-styled repositioning of twelve of them will be summarized in this section.

Repositioning into the Family Dietitian Life-Style

1. Product: Analog Food

Original Positioning: A synthetic health food. Chief benefits were that it was free from carcinogenic chemical additives used to preserve the natural product, it was nonperishable, required no refrigeration, and was several hundred percent less expensive.

Life-Styled Repositioning: A main meal and salad enhancer for the family dietitian in her role as culinary artisan.

2. Service: Fast Food Service

Original Positioning: A substitute eating and entertainment option to periodically replace in-home eating. Chief benefits were convenience, economy, and shared family fun.

Life-Styled Repositioning: A menu planning option for the family dietitian in her role as ongoing meal balancer and daily menu planner.

3. Service: Cooking Schools

Original Positioning: An elitist learning experience for the serious gourmet or frequent party-giver by introducing her to exotic foreign recipes. Chief benefits were pride, prestige, and self-image improvement.

Life-Styled Repositioning: A daily menu planning supplement for the family dietitian in her role as food selector, meal balancer, and food stylist.

Repositioning into the Personal Health Care Manager Life-Style

4. Product: Self-Diagnostic Kits

Original Positioning: Illness-detection tools for sick people. Chief benefit was displacement of need for professional medical services and their attendant fees in crisis situations.

Life-Styled Repositioning: A health-maintenance product for the personal health care manager in her role as family physical health guardian and educator.

5. Product: Skin-Care Products

Original Positioning: A medical product line of cleansers and moisturizers created from a secret European formula to restore healthful conditions to teenaged skin and delay the aging process for mature women. Chief benefits were natural ingredients, a prescribed schedule of application, and the mystique imported to the product line by its European creator.

Life-Styled Repositioning: A beauty care product line for every personal beauty care manager in her role as socially attractive woman.

Repositioning into the Environmental Manager Life-Style

6. Product: Home Craft Kits

Original Positioning: A line of challenging creative projects for women who like to sew, knit, and crochet. Chief benefits were unique designs and a reasonably high degree of difficulty, and therefore a high sense of personal reward and acclaim.

Life-Styled Repositioning: A simple, do-it-yourself home furnishing and decoration line for the environmental manager in her role as cottage craftsman.

7. Product: Home Fire Alarm

Original Positioning: A high-technology smoke and heat detector that protects property and life. Chief benefits were scientific construction based on sophisticated engineering technology, dependability, and automatic capability.

Life-Styled Repositioning: A life insurance product for the environmental manager in her role as family safety director.

8. Service: Automobile Maintenance

Original Positioning: A car care service for preventive auto maintenance and repair. Chief benefits were professional care, pick-up and delivery services, and guaranteed satisfaction.

Life-Styled Repositioning: A car-care educational service and do-it-yourself repair clinic for minor repairs, allied to a professional diagnostic and repair service, for the environmental manager in her role as automobile repair and maintenance manager.

Repositioning into the Travel and Entertainment Manager Life-Style

9. Service: Leisure Time Services

Original Positioning: A consultation service to recommend jet-set leisure-experience activities for affluent, highly experienced consumers of discretionary time. Chief benefits were the promise of unique, one-of-a-kind trips, visits, and activities with high enjoyment and envy values.

Life-Styled Repositioning: Advice, recommendations, and suggested agendas for the optional use of everyday discretionary time by the environmental manager in her leisure planning roles as family travel agent and family entertainment director.

10. Product: Video Games

Original Positioning: A home entertainment adjunct to the television set. Chief benefits were extended use of TV set, added family fun, and long-term use.

Life-Styled Repositioning. A new entertainment medium whose values exceed and are independent of television to meet the needs of the environmental manager in her role of amusement selector, leisure planner, toy and game buyer.

Repositioning into the Training and Education Manager Life-Style

11. Product: Cat Food

Original Positioning: A cat food line. Chief benefits were convenience, nutrition, and good taste.

Life-Styled Repositioning: A food and accessory product-service system to help the training manager use food as a training aid in her role as pet feeder and teacher.

Repositioning in the Family Business Manager Life-Style

12. Product: Home Computers

Original Positioning: A minicomputer and accompanying software programs. Chief benefits were multiple uses for homemaker in the household and family schoolwork along with reasonable price and advanced technology.

Life-Styled Repositioning: A pay-for-itself credit management tool and budget planner for the family business manager in her role as household money manager.

3

Life-Styling to Create New Product Opportunities in a Specific Field

The process of creating a range of new product opportunities in a specific field is a highly cost-effective management policy. As many companies have discovered, it can help minimize new product risk and maximize profit opportunities. There is a third reason for its cost-effectiveness: It can make a significant contribution to amortizing the investment that is always involved in learning about a market and establishing an ongoing franchise in it.

The decision to attempt the development of related product groups in one interconnected field is an effort to spread the cost of market franchise initiation and maintenance over the broadest possible product base. It can be regarded, too, as a method of utilizing more fully a market's existing acceptance of the company as its prime supplier. The central factor in deriving this benefit is to establish a corporate identity as a *supplier to a specific field* of common attitude and activity patterns rather than as a supplier of specific products. In this way, a company can help its new product development program by positioning itself in a comprehensive manner: as a supplier to the comprehensive life-style of home environment management, for example, instead of as a manufacturer of a scattered list of individual products such as plate glass picture windows, household paints, and ceramic cooking surfaces for kitchen ranges. Similarly, another company can approach its market as a preemptive supplier to many of the broad needs of the family physician market instead of as a narrowly defined manufacturer of feminine hygiene products. In both cases, the umbrella of market acceptance that can be created in this manner can provide a ready-made framework for each new product to hang onto as it enters its life-styled market.

Life-styling a market's definition in this way can give it what, perhaps paradoxically, may be thought of as a breadth of unity. The market can be seen as a unit, having a cohesive pattern of attitudes and activities. Yet within its unity, it offers a breadth of diverse new product opportunities which can have a strong marketing relationship to one another.

Relating new product opportunities to a specific field is a common problem in business growth and diversification. A company which bases its growth policy on the principle of agglomeration rather than conglomeration faces the problem continually. Its management wants the interrelated type of product line structure whose individual elements add up to the same overall definition of what business the company is in. Yet more and more intensive exploitation of any given product line has probably come to be increasingly difficult under traditional ways of seizing the concept of its business. New insights can often be gained in this kind of situation by life-styling the field which is under inquiry and then deriving related new manufacturing and marketing functions from it.

Exhibit 9. Risk analysis of technical applications to markets.

Lowest Risk	**1** Established Technology Applied Against an Established Market	**2** Established Technology Applied Against a New Market
	3 New Technology Applied Against an Established Market	**4** New Technology Applied Against a New Market	**Highest Risk**

Very often when this is done, a company will come to the realization that it has on hand only a portion of the technologies required to serve the comprehensive needs of a life-style. This prevents it from entering into potentially profitable new product opportunities for which a life-styling fit already exists and whose market has a reservoir of acceptance for the company as a supplier. This realization is not always easy to translate into remedial action. A major problem lies in the fact that installing a new technology in an ongoing business, either by internal development or by acquisition from outside, is a hazardous undertaking.

As Exhibit 9 shows, linking new technologies with an established market is a more difficult process than continuing to serve an established market with an established technology. In most cases, it is more difficult by at least a factor of two. But since the market remains familiar to the company, this course of action is saved from even greater risk. As soon as new markets are brought into consideration, the difficulty increases sharply. Applying an existing technology to a new market can entail as much as a fourfold increase in difficulty over applying it to an established market. The ultimate hazard, of course, is to attempt the simultaneous integration of both a new technology and a new market. In this type of situation it can be as much as 16 times more difficult than the initial situation of directing an established science toward established customers.

Despite these predictable obstacles, innovative technologies must increasingly be adopted by most manufacturers if their new product opportunities are to be fully realized. Many of the risks with new sciences can be squeezed out in advance if a company's established markets have first been life-styled. This can make it a good deal easier from an organizational point of view to incorporate a new science into the company's existing functional mix. It can also help the new science's market performance to become more quickly successful. Because all the new products in the company's innovative stream will be impinging on a common life-styled market, their technological diversity will remain largely an internal fact. Out in the marketplace where it counts, the fact of the matter is that the uncommonly derived products will possess a common marketing rationale since they fit together into a system that serves a unified life-style. Thus, from a market's point of view, a multitechnology company which serves a common life-style can still come across as a unified supplier.

In the remainder of this chapter, a developer's thought process will be sketched out as he life-styles the foundation for new product opportunities issuing from the major market role of family physician. As he does so, two fundamental principles will become apparent: One is the astonishing variety and depth of opportunity that can reside within a life-style role; the other is the typical need for complementary technologies to be added to the corporate capability if a full range of life-styled marketing opportunities is to be realized.

Life-Styling New Product Opportunities
for the Family Physician

The developer's company in this case history has traditionally defined its business as *feminine hygiene*. Under this concept of mission, its management manufactured internal and external protective products: tampons, sanitary napkins, and their accessories. It also furnished a market information and education service which was supplied without charge to pre-teenage and teenage girls or their mothers. For several generations, its new product activities had been confined to marginal renovations of existing products, such as a more absorbent tampon or a more comfortable napkin. Its first deviations from this practice were to market a feminine deodorant line to be used in conjunction with its basic products and a feminine analgesic for the relief of occasional pain.

In life-styled terms, it is clear that this manufacturer has really been serving only a part of that small segment of the family physician market which needs personal care. The specific nature of this aspect of care makes it naturally self-limiting for new product development: Not only is the use situation a limited entity in itself; even more importantly, it is a rather small part of the family physician lifestyle and its component roles.

In Exhibit 10, five of the family physician's component roles are shown in a manner worked out with Karl Aldinger (on behalf of Kimberly-Clark). Four of them are within the existing orbit of the company, but in no case is any role more than slightly encompassed. Although this does not, of course, preclude profitability, it does suggest considerable unserved opportunity. One additional role is not encompassed at all. Yet all five roles can easily be brought into a new orbital sphere, represented in the exhibit by the double circle, once a life-styling approach to

Exhibit 10.   Life-style roles encompassed by two different corporate definitions.

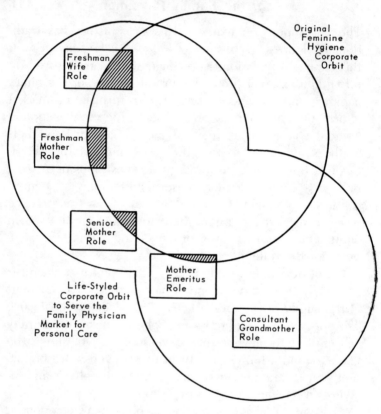

diversification has been adopted and the family physician role has been defined in its entirety for the company's purposes.

When a business of this sort begins to consider its market in a life-styled manner, a true broadening of its new product opportunities can take place. Once the company realizes that it has been an accepted supplier of long standing to one segment of the family physician market, the natural direction for developmental effort to take is to diversify this original foothold. The developer's central question then becomes, "What other related areas of the family physician market can be exploited commercially by our existing or acquirable technologies?"

In order to answer this question, the new product developer will have to undertake a three-part program.

First, he will have to dissect the family physician life-style in order to define its component roles that offer prime market opportunities. The most practical way for him to do this is by life-cycling the needs of the family physician so that he will be able to see them in the context of their time of occurrence.

Second, he will have to pinpoint the commercial opportunities which may be inherent in the needs of the family physician's life-style at each station of her life cycle.

Third, he will have to assign a priority to each interface where a major need takes place at a life-cycle station. This will provide him with a sense of urgency about his new product and with service opportunities in their proper rank ordering of promised profit.

In the following pages, these three parts of the developer's program to create a range of related product opportunities growing out of a life-style role will be examined sequentially. Their examination proceeds through phase 9 where need gaps have become apparent to the developer, where he has conceived of new product and service ideas to meet them, and where he has put priorities on the rank order of their development (see Exhibit 11).

Life-Cycling the Family Physician's Needs for New Products

In Chapter 2, the commercial life of the beer drinker was cycled through its major chronological stations. These sta-

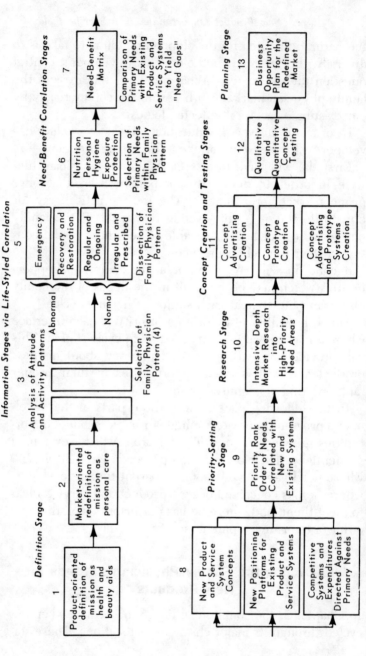

Exhibit 11. Life-styled market structuring plan.

tions provide convenient time frames for evaluating the patterns of attitudes and activities that can compose life-style roles. We know that some roles occur only once in a commercial lifetime. Other roles are recurrent, appearing at several life-cycle stations. At each recurrence, certain aspects of the life-style remain the same while other aspects emerge or disappear. The life-style role of family physician is an example of a recurring attitude and activity pattern that undergoes important commercial changes on a station-to-station basis throughout a married woman homemaker's life cycle.

The life cycle of the family physician is illustrated in Exhibit 12. Five major phases are highlighted for their commercial significance. In chronological order, they are:

1. *Freshman wife,* which encompasses the married woman homemaker from the age of 18 to 24 whose family physicianship is practiced on her husband, herself, and their pets.
2. *Freshman mother,* which encompasses the married woman homemaker from the age of 20 to 35 whose family physicianship has been expanded to include children under the age of 6.
3. *Senior mother,* which encompasses the married woman homemaker from the age of 30 to 49 whose family physicianship is practiced on herself, her husband, her children between the ages of 6 and 17, their pets, and perhaps her parents and in-laws.
4. *Mother emeritus,* which encompasses the married woman homemaker from the age of 40 to 65 whose children are over 18 and whose family physicianship is once again principally confined to her husband, herself, and perhaps her pets.
5. *Consultant grandmother,* which encompasses the married woman homemaker from the age of 40 to 65

Exhibit 12.   The family physician life cycle.

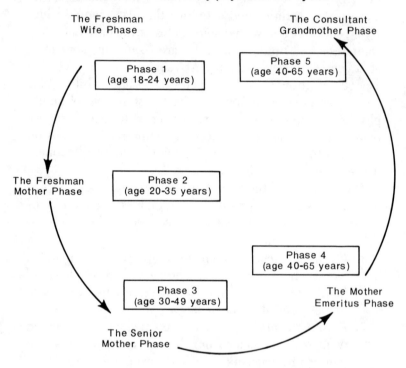

whose family physicianship is practiced on herself, her children, her grandchildren, and perhaps her pets.

These life-cycle phases will be well populated in the United States throughout the decade of the 1980s. In phase 1 it is expected there will be two to three million freshman wives with commercializable family physician needs. The freshman mothers in phase 2 may total between 12 and 15 million women. Senior mothers in phase 3 will probably be an even larger group, perhaps accounting for 15 to 18 million women, with the greatest number in the 35- to 44-year age range. Phases 4 and 5 combined have the potential of containing 30 million mothers emeritus and consultant grandmothers.

At each life-cycle station, the developer will find many new product opportunities growing out of the homemaker's passage through each phase of her physician-playing role. The following summary of several leading aspects of these life-style roles, and some of the major product needs they suggest, was worked out with Vic Kweller, Bart Panettiere, and Lorraine Scarpa (on behalf of General Foods). Two conclusions quickly became clear: Each life-style role is a complex, interrelated market in itself, and each gross product and service opportunity it reveals can become the basis for a sizable business.

Phase 1: Freshman Wife Phase of Family Physician

Major Aspects of Life-Style Role

Emphasis is on expediency, not planning or insurance against illness or accident probabilities. Sporadic remedial care is relied on to keep the body operating. Abuse is accepted, even sought as a challenge, in the knowledge that emergency care will relieve symptoms quickly. Care is therefore principally in the form of first aid and packaged remedies. Preventive medicine is rarely practiced. The freshman wife's major concern is with outward cosmetic appearance—the look of health—more than with inner health itself.

Major Product Needs Derived from Life-Style Role

Head cold remedies
Headache and hangover remedies
Stomach distress remedies
Diet-control aids

Fatigue remedies and sleep inducers
Muscle relaxants and analgesics
Birth-control aids
Feminine hygiene aids
First-aid products
Sleep inhibitors
Quick-energy pickups
Outdoor athletic aids and preventives against insect bites or sunburn

Phase 2: Freshman Mother Phase of Family Physician

Major Aspects of Life-Style Role

Emphasis is on child care, which consumes extraordinary amounts of time and nervous energy. Freshman mother's physician role is principally preventive. As a surrogate resident physician, she acts as her medical doctor's eyes and ears to transmit early warning signs of deviation from health norms: temperature changes, food intake or elimination variances, or rash. The freshman mother is traditionally insecure in her role, hence is almost totally dependent on professional and commercial medical advice with assist from consultant grandmother.

Major Product Needs Derived from Life-Style Role

Baby sick-care disposable kits
Baby foods and feeding accessories
Baby sleeping accessories
Teething aids
Toilet-training aids
Bathing aids
Games and toys, especially stressing dexterity and coordination
Information and education systems

Secondary Aspects of Life-Style Role

Subordinate emphasis is on self-care in order to maintain viability as child-carer and sense of selfhood as compensation for threat of role-submergence. Self-abuse of freshman wife phase is abandoned in favor of prevention, preservation, and restoration.

Secondary Product Needs Derived from Life-Style Role

Vitamins and food supplements
Energy builders
Exercisers
Sleep inducers and regulators
Diet-control aids
Birth-control aids
Feminine hygiene aids

Phase 3: Senior Mother Phase of Family Physician

Major Aspects of Life-Style Role

Emphasis of the senior mother is still on child care, although her dependence on the doctor is progressively lessened as children mature. Diagnosis and remedial action are easier since two-way communication with children is now possible. As children's environment broadens from home to include the school and community, communicable diseases and epidemics may become problems. School and community health authorities take over some maternal responsibilities for health care and illness prevention. Children also assume increasingly independent attitudes and activities relating to self-care. Many of these attitudes are taught by the media and advertising.

Major Product Needs Derived from Life-Style Role

Nutritional food products
Preventive and remedial drugs

Vitamins and food supplements
Diet-control aids
Medical and dental checkups
Soaps
First-aid products
Birth-control aids
Feminine hygiene aids

Secondary Aspects of Life-Style Role

Subordinate emphasis is on self-care, relief of symptoms of aging, and overexertion or overindulgence in recapturing youth. Fear of terminal disease entities becomes recurrent.

Secondary Product Needs Derived from Life-Style Role

Tension relievers
Sleep inducers and inhibitors
Balms and analgesics
Energy and vitality restorers
Authoritative information and consultation services

Phase 4: Mother Emeritus Phase of Family Physician

Major Aspects of Life-Style Role

Emphasis is on renewed self-care and care of husband and grandparents now that children have matured. Psychological problems occur, especially as discretionary time increases and husband-wife tensions accumulate. Geriatric problems begin, and onset of menopause brings emotional difficulties. Resumption of career by mother emeritus may also renew anxieties, induce stress or exposure to communicable diseases. At the same time she is caring for grandparents, mother emeritus may require role-reversing care by her children.

Major Product Needs Derived from Life-Style Role
Information services on terminal diseases
Rejuvenation aids
Health foods
Diet-control aids
Feminine hygiene aids
Vitamins and food supplements
Tension relievers
Physical supporters

Phase 5: Consultant Grandmother Phase of Family Physician

Major Aspects of Life-Style Role
Emphasis is on self-care and care of grandchildren. As babysitter, consultant grandmother acts as mother surrogate in administering child-care products and services. She also performs educational and supportive functions during pregnancy of her daughter or daughter-in-law.

Major Product Needs Derived from Life-Style Role
Health foods
Diet-control aids
Vitamins and food supplements
Physical supporters

Pinpointing New Product Opportunities for the Family Physician

Once a life-style role has been cycled through its time stations, the developer's next step is to examine the gross needs that can be generated by each phase of a life role and to use those needs as a means of stimulating his thinking about highly specific product and service concepts. In

Exhibit 13, five situations that regularly recur in the freshman mother phase of the family physician life-style have been charted. Two of these situations, classified as normal patterns, are principally diagnostic and preventive by nature. The three remaining situations are abnormal patterns of attitudes and activities. They are emergency or restorative, requiring intensive activity on the part of the freshman mother or prolonged attention to recovery from an emergency situation that has been dealt with successfully.

To show how new product and service concepts can be pulled out of a specific time station within a life-style role, the "Norm 2" category of normal situations for the freshman mother has been isolated from Exhibit 13 and inten-

Exhibit 13.   Marketable situations recurring in the freshman mother phase of the family physician life-style role.

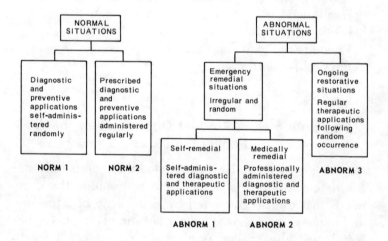

sively analyzed for marketable ideas, according to a method developed with Peter Karp.

First of all, the developer must get inside the Norm 2 use situation and structure it. To do so, he must ask himself, "What are the component parts of this situation that make it tick?" He already knows that it is composed of regular ongoing diagnostic and preventive applications of products and services ("regular" in this case meaning daily or weekly). Now he must identify the needs that require these diagnostic and preventive applications. When he has done that, he will have a target list of potential commercial opportunities.

If the developer follows the Karp method, he will be able to pinpoint eight major needs from within the "Norm 2" use situation of the family physician role as it is played by married women homemakers during their freshman mother phase:

1. The need to guarantee a sufficient amount of *rest and sleep* among children and other family members.

2. The need to generate a sufficient amount of *exercise* among children and other family members.

3. The need to provide proper *nutrition* to ensure the health of children and other family members.

4. The need to provide *sanitation* and *germ or pest control* in the household environment.

5. The need to teach proper *personal hygiene* practices to children and other family members.

6. The need to provide *exposure protection* against outdoor hazards for children and other family members.

7. The need to provide *safety protection* among children and other family members.

8. The need for the homemaker to receive *reassuring*

> *feedback* that tells her she is being a competent family health manager and helps dispel her normal fears and doubts.

After a need situation such as Norm 2 has been structured anatomically as in Exhibit 13, the developer must then take on the job that Karp calls "need stripping"—a process very much like peeling a banana—in which each need area is stripped of its pretenses so that its chief susceptibilities to product benefits can be uncovered.

Need stripping will very likely flood the developer's mind with an inflow of product and service concepts ranging from the obvious to the exotic. The developer should record all his concepts in the manner of a reporter who is taking testimony from a market and not as an editor of it. Critical judgment and validation can and must come later. At this stage, the developer's intent should be to get himself into a frame of mind that will permit him to "vibrate" sympathetically with his need analysis. He will know when he has reached this state of resonance because the phenomenon of "reinvention" will begin to occur. As this happens, the developer will find himself making recurrent discoveries of the original reason for existence of many companies and their product lines. He will, in short, be reliving their invention as each comes to his awareness. The more companies and products the developer's analysis reveals, the greater assurance he can have that he is tuned in to his market and that he is examining its needs in a realistic way. For example, developers who analyze the need situation classified as Abnorm 1 in Exhibit 13 inevitably uncover the genesis of Johnson & Johnson as a supplier to this market and of its Band-Aids brand as a highly marketable answer to the need for convenient, disposable, and self-administered first-aid treatment.

In the Norm 2 situation, whose needs are stripped in the following list, the reason for being of Johnson & Johnson will be confirmed several times, as will the origins of many products of Procter & Gamble, Colgate-Palmolive, Kimberly-Clark, and dozens of others. As the developer uses the reinvention phenomenon to sharpen his sensitivities to the many ways by which life-styled market needs have created existing product demand, he ought to be able to raise his batting average in generating new product concepts that do not yet exist but that are called for by his own market's living roles.

(Needs) *Attitude and Activity Patterns*	*(Benefits)* *Product and Service System Concepts*
1. Need to generate sufficient *rest and sleep* among family members	◆ Information and good habit training
1.1 Children's need for a full 10–12 hours' sleep nightly	◆ Proper bedding (sheets, pillowcases)
◆ To provide mental alertness/eliminate nervousness or irritation	
◆ To provide growth and energy	◆ Proper air circulation and heating (humidifiers, air conditioners, heaters, ionizers, room decongestants)
◆ To protect against illness and low body resistance	◆ Proper sound controls (soundproofing, earmuffs, music, clock radios, "white sound" noise makers)
	◆ Controlled late-night eating habits (hot drinks, digestible snacks)
	◆ Presleep hot bath pattern (bath products/toys, quick-bath substitutes, heat pads)

(Needs)
Attitude and Activity Patterns

(Benefits)
Product and Service System Concepts

- Lighting and room colors (curtains and shades, graphics, color effects)
- Tension eliminators and sleep inducers (media, books, toys, fear-dispellers, self-control aids)
- Light-exercise program (instructions and equipment)
- Information and good habit training

1.2 Children's need for afternoon naps
- As in 1.1, *plus* need to extend day for child beyond normal pattern (convenience sleep)

1.3 Adult need for 6–8 hours' sleep nightly

- Convenience-sleep products (drugs or specially designed products from array in 1.1)
- Sleeping aids (prescription or nonprescription)

1.4 Adult need for nap or convenience sleep or sleep-need eliminator
- Special activity needs (driving, round-the-clock work need)

- Information and good habit training

- Convenience-sleep products
- Quick-energy pills and stay-awake pills

2. Need to generate sufficient *exercise* among family members

2.1 Child/adult needs for more energy before or during exercise

- Gatorade-type food products
- Vitamins, minerals, food supplements
- Special meal preparation (restorative snack products)

2.2 Child/adult needs for restorative pickup after exercise

- Vitamins, minerals, food supplements
- Information and good habit training

2.3 Need to establish normal child/adult exercise pattern
- To provide mental alertness; eliminate nervousness or irritation
- To provide growth and energy

- Leisure-time activities
- Athletic equipment purchases or rental
- Pools and saunas

(Needs) *Attitude and Activity Patterns*	(Benefits) *Product and Service System Concepts*
◆ To improve strength and endurance ◆ To improve ability, dexterity, and coordination	◆ Enrollment in exercise activity programs ◆ Active and passive exercise salons ◆ Health-rationalized travel and entertainment (spas, warm-weather areas, resorts)
◆ To provide mental confidence	◆ Health-rationalized major purchases (boats, campers)
◆ To improve lungs and oxygen system	◆ Special exercise for development of specific skills (dexterity, coordination, manipulation)
◆ To protect against illness and low bodily resistance ◆ To deter bodily deterioration ◆ To ensure proper weight control 2.4 Child/adult need for exercise	
◆ As in 2.3 *plus* symptom of need (tires easily)	◆ Information and good habit training ◆ Vitamins, minerals, food supplements ◆ Product and service systems to encourage enrollment in special competitive-reward programs
2.5 Fear of getting hurt or sick while exercising	◆ Protective clothing, equipment, accessories ◆ Information and safety precaution aids ◆ Remedial products (Band-Aid type)
2.6 Fear of overexercising, leading to health problem	◆ Information and safety precaution aids ◆ Systems of self-monitoring and determining how much is enough ◆ Remedial products (Ben-Gay type)

(Needs)
Attitude and Activity Patterns

(Benefits)
Product and Service System Concepts

2.7 Old people's need to exercise but fear of geriatric limitations and dangers

♦ Information and safety precaution aids
♦ Systems of self-monitoring and determining how much is enough
♦ Light exercise (jogger syndrome)

2.8 Making work therapeutic exercise

♦ Information and programs
♦ Redesign of relevant products to aid in therapeutic program

2.9 Special exercise programs for pregnancy (can be considered within normal framework)

♦ Information and programs
♦ Special exercise equipment and aids

3. Need to provide proper *nutrition* to ensure health of family members
3.1 Special dietary considerations during pregnancy
♦ To ensure proper physical and mental development from embryonic stage
(Regular supervised prenatal program can be considered within normal framework)

♦ Medical/paramedical information aids
♦ Increased levels of food intake (protein)
♦ Vitamins, minerals, food supplements
♦ Nutrition program (five light meals per day optimum, with special portion-controlled foods)

3.2 Special dietary considerations during period of lactation
3.3 Special dietary considerations for infant prior to table-foods stage

♦ Medical/paramedical information aids
♦ Medical/paramedical information aids
♦ Baby foods and special formulas (protein)
♦ Vitamin, mineral, food supplement insurance
♦ Nutrition program with clinical control possibility

(*Needs*) *Attitude and Activity Patterns*	(*Benefits*) *Product and Service System Concepts*
3.4 Child/adult needs for more energy before and during activities	• Gatorade-type food products • Vitamins, minerals, food supplements
3.5 Child/adult needs for restorative pickup after activities	• Special meal preparation (restorative snack products) • Vitamins, minerals, food supplements
3.6 Need for extra insurance against dietary deficiencies (in normal health situations)	• Information aids on nutrition and menu planning • Good habit training aids • Authoritarian aids to support difficult implementation role
• To ensure mental alertness	
• To ensure growth and energy	• Vitamins, minerals, food supplements
• To protect against illness and low bodily resistance	• Regular food products with nutritive edge • Health-designed new food products (high protein) • Health-faddist/cult products • Nutritive program opportunity (five-light-meal system, snack products)
3.7 Need to compensate for bad eating habits	• Information and good habit training • Vitamins, minerals, food supplements • New sweet-treat product line (high protein)
3.8 Need for healthful, convenient, light snack meals for on-the-run situations (work, activity, play, travel, as in 3.6)	• Replacements for coffee-and-doughnuts syndrome • New products for convenient light meals on the run
3.9 Strong concern for food purity	• Health foods and organic foods • Health-designed new food products

(Needs)
Attitude and Activity Patterns

(Benefits)
Product and Service System Concepts

3.10 Dietary restrictions other than physiological (vegetarian, etc.)

◆ Meatless food lines

3.11 Weight-watching for cosmetic reasons (normal, nonobesity situations)

◆ Weight maintenance (slight gain or loss)

3.12 Special dietary situations

◆ Metrecal syndrome
◆ Diet control through systematic food intake plans and programs
◆ Sweet-treats (high protein, low calorie)
Ingredient substitutes (saccharin)
Line of specially designed control foods:
◆ To encourage bodily functions (regularity, potency)
◆ To encourage bodily effects (clearer skin, better hair control and pigmentation)
◆ To encourage growth, agility, and endurance
◆ To encourage mental alertness and clarity
◆ To retard chronic ailments and degeneration processes
◆ To effect longevity
◆ To create or sustain special moods

4. Need for proper *sanitation and germ/pest control* in household environment

4.1 Garbage handling and disposal

◆ Disposable protection and removal products (gloves, pails, bags, carts)
◆ Disposal units
◆ Disinfectants (sprays, medicated soaps)

4.2 Baby toilet training

◆ Disposable protection and removal products (gloves, diapers, bedding)

(Needs) Attitude and Activity Patterns	*(Benefits)* Product and Service System Concepts
	◆ Disinfectants (sprays, medicated soaps)
4.3 Pet toilet training	◆ Disposable protection and removal products (bags, scoops, gloves)
	◆ Disinfectants (sprays, powders)
4.4 Bathroom cleaning	◆ Self-cleaning products for toilets
	◆ Disinfectants (sprays, wicks, electrical air cleaners, ionizers)
4.5 Refrigerator cleaning	◆ Self-cleaning products for refrigerators and freezers
	◆ Disinfectants (sprays, ionizers, wicks)
	◆ Food preservatives
4.6 After-meal food cleanup	◆ Disposables
	◆ Soaps, sprays
4.7 Clothes cleaning	◆ Medicated cleaning sprays
	◆ Disposable brushes, pads
4.8 Shoe-carried problems	◆ Disposable doormats and floormats
	◆ Disinfectants
4.9 Bug and pest control	◆ Sprays, traps
	◆ Insect-repellent lotions, sprays

5. Need to generate proper *personal hygiene* practices among family members

5.1 Proper tooth and mouth care	◆ Information, good habit training, authoritarian aids
◆ To protect against decay and loss of teeth	◆ Toothbrushes, toothpaste, powder, and kits
◆ To control mouth germs and odors	◆ Mouthwashes, gargles
◆ To enhance appearance (cosmetic concern)	◆ Cleaning sprays, dental floss
◆ To reduce dental pain	◆ Control of intake of sugar and sweets

(Needs)
Attitude and Activity Patterns

(Benefits)
Product and Service System Concepts

♦ Chewing gum and after-meal "candies" to break up plaque formations

5.2 Prevention of body odors (excluding teeth)
♦ To protect against perspiration and wetness

♦ Information and good habit training
♦ Bath and shower habits and products
♦ Bath substitutes

♦ To control odor emission
♦ To enhance appearance (cosmetic concern)

♦ Soaps (regular, medicated)
♦ Deodorants, antiperspirants
♦ Feminine hygiene sprays, powders
♦ Foot sprays

5.3 Skin cleanliness
♦ To eliminate dirt, germs
♦ To enhance appearance (cosmetic concern)

♦ Information and good habit training
♦ Bath, shower, and wash-up habits
♦ Soaps (regular, medicated)
♦ Disinfectants

5.4 Convenience sponge bath
5.5 Monthly menstrual care (normal)
♦ Pain relief
♦ Flow control
♦ Protection in social situations

♦ Bath substitutes
♦ Drug products
♦ Napkin-type products
♦ Tampon-type insertion products
♦ Combination napkin-tampon products
♦ Feminine hygiene sprays

5.6 Hair and dandruff control (normal)
♦ To protect scalp
♦ To control hair
♦ To eliminate dirt and germs
♦ To enhance appearance (cosmetic concern)
5.7 Hair removal and shaving control

♦ Hair shampoos, fixatives
♦ Hair tonics, creams
♦ Dandruff-control additives

♦ Shaving preparations and accessories

(Needs)
Attitude and Activity Patterns

(Benefits)
Product and Service System Concepts

- To control dirt and germs
- To enhance appearance (cosmetic concern)

5.8 Hand care
- To protect
- To control nail splitting, skin flaking
- To enhance appearance (cosmetic concern)

5.9 Sexual hygiene
- To protect
- To control
- To procreate

- Depilatories

- Rubber or disposable gloves
- Hand lotions, creams

- Information and training
- Clinics
- Pills, contraceptives
- Menstruation-related products
- Menopause-related products

6. Need to provide proper *exposure protection* among family members

6.1 In-home air conditioning
- Adequate heat
- Adequate coolness
- Adequate air flow

6.2 Indoor/outdoor clothing systems
- Adequate protection against cold and wetness

6.3 Sun-protective coatings and products

6.4 Bug protection
6.5 Wind protection
6.6 Air or water pollution prevention

6.7 Plant protection, weed killers

- Heating systems
- Fans, air conditioners
- Room humidifiers, decongestants
- Air purifiers

- Clothing, coats, boots, rainwear
- Thermometers, barometers

- Preparations
- Other sun precautions
- Salt pills
- Insect repellants, sprays
- Chapstick-type products
- Pollution diagnosis equipment
- Oxygen inhalators
- Sprays
- Allergy controllers (normal)

(Needs)
Attitude and Activity Patterns

(Benefits)
Product and Service System Concepts

7. Need to provide proper *safety, hazard protection*
7.1 Need to poison-proof the home
♦ Child-proof

♦ Information and good habit training
♦ Drugs, medicine storage systems
♦ Household cleansers/polishers storage systems
♦ Insecticides, garden sprays storage systems
♦ Toiletries, cosmetics storage systems
♦ Fuels, paints, and preservatives storage systems

7.2 Eliminate sharp objects
7.3 Protect against guns, rifles
7.4 Protect against electricity
7.5 Street, yard, bicycle safety monitoring

♦ Information and good habit training

7.6 Need for penal-type walls
♦ Ways to "protectively imprison" children
7.7 Automotive safety

♦ Indoor and outdoor pens and playhouses
♦ Cribs, highchairs
♦ Garage doors and car storage systems
♦ Carbon monoxide protection

7.8 Special work clothing
7.9 Protect against habit-forming drugs

♦ Goggles, gloves
♦ Information and good habit training

8. Need of family health manager for *two-way feedback,* **instilling confidence and dispelling fears and puzzlements**
8.1 Self-diagnosis of health
♦ Absence of illness or repetitive illness patterns
♦ Appearance of health: size, strength, figure, complexion, posture (*not* frail, anemic, sickly, fat, pudgy)

♦ Information and media feedback

(*Needs*)	(*Benefits*)
Attitude and Activity Patterns	*Product and Service System Concepts*

◆ Activity effects: alertness, calmness, energy, endurance, growth, confidence, athletic prowess
◆ Peer comparison: looks equally fit/better fit than friends
8.2 Peer diagnosis of health, as in 8.1
8.3 Institutional feedback of health

◆ Information and media feedback
◆ School systems, business organizations (history, records of achievement)

8.4 Medical or paramedical diagnosis of health
8.5 Need to supplement regular periodic medical diagnosis

◆ M.D.s, diagnostic clinics, dentists, etc.
◆ Information and good habits
◆ In-home self-diagnostic kits

Assigning Priorities to New Product Opportunities for the Family Physician

The concept of the life cycle is based on the assumption that the needs of a customer playing a life-style role will change as he or she moves through successive age stations. While certain needs may arise only at specific stations, we have seen how other needs, such as many of those in the normal category known as Norm 2, can recur at several phases of the family physician life-style. But their importance will differ, and they are far more demanding at some life-cycle phases than at others. Wherever they assume a high degree of importance, the developer has the right to believe that an above-average opportunity can exist for profitable new product commercialization. He must therefore place top priority on such an opportunity and hold in abeyance lesser claims on his resources.

The act of assigning priorities is one of the most crucial steps in the new product development process. If no priorities are set, the developer will often find himself trying to push several projects along simultaneously or—even worse over the long range—working only on projects that he himself or someone in upper management personally favors. Yet if the wrong priorities are set, the allocation of corporate resources to the development process can be hopelessly confused. Projects of small potential payout, or of no payout at all, may be given precedence over winners. Competition may perceive key need gaps faster and move to fill them preemptively so that the developer will have to settle for an enduring second or third position if he is not to be frozen out of a market entirely. Thus the entire future cash flow of his company may be damaged and its historical market and product profiles detrimentally altered.

Assigning priorities to new product opportunities that emerge from need stripping can be a rather complex process, as Appendix B will show, or it can be based on the relatively simple method illustrated in Exhibit 14. In the exhibit, the eight major needs within the freshman mother's Norm 2 situation have been organized in a matrix with the five life-cycle stations of the family physician role. At each interface where a need meets a life station, a number has been set down to express the developer's combined subjective and objective estimate of the commercial viability of the need at that particular station. In the numbering scheme used, 1 is low and 5 indicates a developmental area of the highest priority.

The information brought out by the matrix, despite its simplified system, can be productively evaluated by two methods. One method is to follow the developer's primary concern and run vertically down the life-cycle station for the freshman mother phase, which occupies the second

Exhibit 14. Priorities of Norm 2 needs throughout the family physician life cycle.

Major Needs within Norm 2 Use Situations	LIFE-CYCLE STATIONS				
	No. 1 Freshman Wife	No. 2 Freshman Mother	No. 3 Senior Mother	No. 4 Mother Emeritus	No. 5 Consultant Grandmother
1. Rest and sleep	1	3	2	2	2
2. Exercise	4	4	4	4	3
3. Nutrition	4	5	4	4	4
4. Sanitation and germ/pest control	1	5	3	3	3
5. Personal hygiene	5	5	4	4	4
6. Exposure protection	4	5	4	4	4
7. Safety protection	4	5	4	4	4
8. Reassuring feedback	1	5	4	4	5

column. This will reveal the specific opportunities which that phase can offer. When this is done, a remarkable map of high-priority needs can be drawn. As the exhibit illustrates, a total of five out of the eight major needs has been given the top priority ranking number of 5: nutrition, sanitation and germ or pest control, exposure protection, safety protection, and the need for reassuring feedback. A sixth need, personal hygiene, has been ranked with a 4. Even if the low end of what can be considered a high-priority ranking is arbitrarily set at 4, the developer has an extensive target list of major needs at his disposal for development.

Because of the unexpected abundance of opportunity in the freshman mother phase, the developer's priority system must enter a second stage of finer tuning. His five top-priority need areas will now have to undergo further rank-ordering. The developer's subjectivity, along with his portfolio of hard market facts, will once again be called into play. To them, he will have to add additional screening criteria, such as the strengths and weaknesses of major corporate capabilities or top management preferences for a specific business image and its financial objectives, in order to place one priority area in the forefront of his action program.

The second method of analyzing the matrix in order to extract helpful information from it is to read it across instead of only down the freshman mother column. In this way, the varying importance of each of the eight need categories can be evaluated in the course of the family physician's progress through her life cycle. For example, the need for sleep never assumes a very high commercial priority at any life-cycle station. It is at its highest importance for the freshman mother and the consultant grandmother, with whom it reaches a maximum rating of 3. Both are likely to accept the inevitability of running a sleep deficit while they are on call to their families. They therefore do not generally seek a commercial remedy for it.

On the other hand, a need such as nutrition is always commercially important to the family physician, as are personal hygiene and exposure protection. In each of these three need areas, vast new product possibilities—indeed, even probable new business entities—can exist, awaiting the developer's release. As the need-stripping exercise shown earlier in this chapter suggests, the developer working on the nutritional needs of the family physician in her Norm 2 situation may trigger the release of new profitability from restorative foods or from a light-meal system, new healthful convenience foods to be eaten on the run, or high-energy foods and beverages to be consumed before or during activities. Among personal hygiene needs, the developer may articulate new product concepts for bath and shower substitutes for cleansing and refreshment, internally taken deodorizers, or new systems for hair growth and removal. Finally, in the need area of exposure protection, product concepts can be generated for a wide range of safeguards from wind, sun, insects, cold and heat extremes, and air or water pollution.

Life-Styling New Product Opportunities in Service Marketing

One of the most rewarding byproducts of life-styled marketing is the increased degree of market orientation it imposes on the development process. A second benefit of equal importance is the emphasis it places on the need to create new products that deliver a true user service rather than simply a newly renovated product form. From the life-styled point of view, only a new product's service benefits are marketable. The physical product itself is regarded as merely a transient delivery vehicle for its service.

Life-styled marketing therefore places the new product developer in the position of acting as a translator for his product's service; that is, he must translate an often intangible service benefit into a tangible product. This means that the developer who works for a service organization can have a much more direct relationship with his market, since he does not have to approach it through a product intermediary. He can create a one-to-one relationship with his market's need for new benefits. An airline offers a revealing example of how a basic service business can be proliferated in this way through life-styled methods.

An airline is essentially in the business of processing bits of information over time. One bit is a passenger.

Another bit is the passenger's luggage. A third bit is a carton of air freight. A fourth bit is the airplane itself. This is a distribution-oriented processing business, and to engage in it, an airline employs two types of distribution media. One is internal—it consists of an electronic data processing capability which moves information bits called facts through highly condensed time periods called nanoseconds and picoseconds. The airline's other distribution medium is the line's aircraft, which compose its external medium. Their capability lies in moving the computer's information bits in their enlarged, more familiar form as people and goods through telescoped time frames—or, as we are more accustomed to think of it, from a place in one time zone to a place in another.

The innovative efforts of major airlines have traditionally been directed to making marginal improvements in the terms or conditions of the traveler's processing experience by means of alterations in the external distribution medium. For the business traveler, who has been the air industry's most profitable market, these improvements have largely been in the interest of added convenience values. Because the airline business is highly competitive, innovative product or service features are quickly imitated to the point where they tend to neutralize each other at a generally higher level of cost.

For the airline market developer, a life-styled approach to the business segment of his customer groups can open up new sources of profitable income by utilizing more fully the airline's twin processing abilities. When this is done, as revealed by the conceptual thinking worked out with James Sowers (on behalf of American Airlines), a number of major life-styles of business people in relation to airline services can be defined. Six of them are illustrated in Exhibit 15. These life-styles may be described as follows:

Exhibit 15. Businessman life-style roles for airline commercialization.

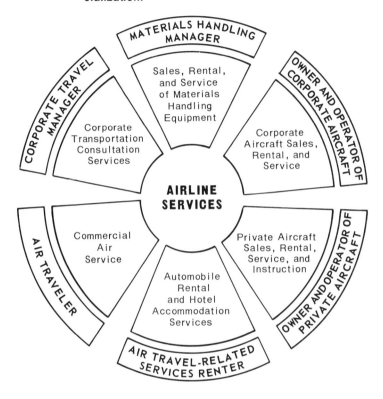

1. *Corporate travel manager,* the businessman's life-style role as a commercial travel planner and arranger for his staff and associates.
2. *Materials handling manager,* the businessman's life-style role as a mover and shipper of goods in the form of air cargo.
3. *Owner and operator of corporate aircraft,* the businessman's life-style role as company air transportation manager.

4. *Air traveler,* the businessman's life-style role as a commercial airline passenger.
5. *Air-travel-related car renter,* the businessman's life-style role as a commercial automobile driver and passenger.
6. *Owner and operator of private aircraft,* the businessman's life-style role as an off-duty flying hobbyist.

Through the practice of need stripping, an airline market development manager can probably find several large targets of opportunity within each of these six roles for the innovative utilization of his company's twin processing capabilities. Existing airline staff and computer capabilities can be combined to form corporate transportation consultation services for the businessman in his role as corporate travel manager. Aircraft can be sold, rented, and serviced to meet the needs of the businessman as owner and operator of corporate and private aircraft, again utilizing existing data processing capabilities. As a third example, automobiles and hotel accommodations can be made available to the air-travel-related renter for continuing his travels or combining business and pleasure. Rental services such as these would also be able to draw on the airline's EDP ability to handle reservations and maintain inventories.

Each of these new service proliferations represents a "new product" concept. In all six examples shown in Exhibit 15, the two main criteria for sound growth are met: the basic business definition of an airline is being maintained or logically extended into closely related opportunities, and the same familiar life-styled market of businessmen is being served—not just by a traditional approach to this market's role as that of commercial air travelers but by a range of interrelated opportunities within a specific field. In the next chapter, we will see how a company which has not yet isolated a specific market target for innovation can do so by means of using life-styling strategies to define even a very broad, vague area of general interest to it. At the same time, we will become aware of how new, logical extensions into related areas of market opportunity can always be within the grasp of the developer.

4

Life-Styling to Create New Product Opportunities in an Area of General Interest

New product development, even in a familiar and relatively specific field, is one of the two highest risk areas of business, along with diversification into vaguely defined new business areas of general interest to the company. Yet a certain vagueness of definition is almost inherent in top management's approach to business diversification into unfamiliar fields. Sometimes this is due to management's indecision about how it really wants to grow or where true growth opportunities can be found. At other times, vaguely defined growth targets may accurately reflect managerial ignorance of any markets but its own. The burden of this indecision or ignorance at the uppermost levels of management eventually falls on the developer. In this way, he inherits a major risk without a commensurate voice in its undertaking.

The main reason for the supreme hazard which accompanies a strategy of undefined or ill-defined diversification is as simple to describe as it is complicated to remedy: vaguely defined areas of general interest offer no structure within which the developer can work and therefore present no easy relationships between what he already knows and what he must learn. It is never the act of learning that is difficult; what is always laborious is providing a structure within which the new knowledge can be meaningfully added to old knowledge.

There are, of course, many strategies for superimposing order on a new product search into a general area in order to come up with major marketing opportunities. Some of these strategies perform better than others, but the skill lies less in the method and more in the developer's sophistication in using it to take a cut at an unknown market area. One common liability which most of these methods share is that they are largely imposed on a market from without rather than dictated by intrinsic patterns within the developer's market itself. This means that they may often match the developer's needs more than his market's needs.

A life-styled method of searching for specific new product opportunities in a loosely indicated area of interest can overcome the liability of being externally applied. In the hands of a market-sensitive developer, life-styling can closely replicate real-world patterns of needs as they actually exist. This can come about if the developer enters the vaguely defined area of general interest with his eye out for attitude and activity pairings, or even the more gross "bundles" of several such pairs, that have a relationship to each other. He must then let the market talk to him—or at least he must listen in on it acutely—and observe the words and behavior it uses to act out its expressions of need.

Marketing Opportunities from Evolving Life-Styles

From the product developer's point of view, just what do we mean by *the market?* For many marketers, the mass middle majority married woman homemaker between the ages of 19 and 39 has been the traditional kingpin (perhaps "queenpin" is a better word) of consumer product and service marketing. She functions as the chief decision maker, leading influencer, and purchasing agent of a small business called the family. To perform these jobs, she assumes as many as a dozen life-style roles. The more personnel the business contains (especially the more children), the broader its range of property holdings, and the more diversified its activities, the more important she is to marketers.

This role model of combination dietitian, nurse, mother, wife, sanitary engineer, and travel and entertainment director remains in the 1980s, as always, a prime marketing target. As a result of the socioeconomic revolutions of the 1960s and 1970s, however, two other roles for women have taken on increasing prominence. One is married women homemakers in their life-style role as careerists. The other is unmarried women in their life-style role as homemakers.

Married Women Homemaker-Careerists

Some married women homemakers are "also careerists"; some married women careerists are "also homemakers." From a marketing point of view, this is merely a question of perception; in both cases, it is the homemaker life-styles that represent the most marketable opportunities.

Many careerist roles for women express attitude and activity patterns that are largely undifferentiated from the career roles of men. In these cases, career demand patterns are career demand patterns regardless of the sex of the careerist. Intellectually, they generate needs for information resources. Physically, they create needs for business clothing and executive paraphernalia such as briefcases and attaché cases that must be tailored to women's tastes and use requirements: "feminized without becoming womanized."

Life-styled roles for women careerists may include some or all of the following:

1. The careerist in her life-styled role as business grooming care manager, a role that generates products and counseling services directed to the care of hands, hair, skin, and face.

2. The careerist in her life-styled role as business clothing systems engineer, a role that creates needs for products and counseling services directed to executive dress management ("success clothes") and accessory selection and wear.

3. The careerist in her life-styled role as business interior environment manager, a role that demands products and counseling services directed to executive office furnishings, decor, and mood styling.

4. The careerist in her life-styled role as business establishment ladder climber, a role that encourages the development of counseling services directed to enabling women to position themselves professionally within the male-dominated business establishment.

Each of these roles, and others such as careerist travel manager and careerist office environment manager, can generate profitable product and service concepts along with strategy directives for marketing them. But it is on the homemaker side, not on the careerist side of their life-styled roles that married women homemakers who go into business set up the most significant needs for new products.

A career makes two kinds of impact on a married woman's homemaking roles. Attitudinally, it can diminish their overall importance, especially for the careerist who is "also a homemaker." A career also condenses the time and reduces the psychic and physical energy available for homemaking. These twin impacts impose a new dimension on product and service development: Speed and ease become the paramount benefits. The ultimate in speed and ease is, of course, not having to think about anything or to do anything at all in a specific aspect of homemaking.

Women homemakers who work are therefore players of the same life-styled roles as women homemakers who do not work, but they are players under pressure. Distraction or lack of interest pressure them, time pressures them, and performance energy requirements pressure them. In their products and services, they need to have more built-in help. More responsibilities have to be taken off their hands. More ease, more speed, more quality control, and greater immediacy of the end result as well as greater availability are basic benefits that must be offered.

These criteria give rise to needs for such timesavers as professional menu-planning and catering services, one-stop shopping or shopping by mail or telephone, and appliances such as dishwashers, trash compactors, self-cleaning ovens and self-defrosting refrigerators, food processors, and microwave ovens. Double-duty utensils that can be used for both cooking and serving are also likely to represent high perceived values along with instant semiprepared nutritious packaged meals.

Sales policies, marketing practices, business ethics, and even legislative fiats come in for renovation under the timesaving pressures that make an impact on married women homemaker–careerists. Products must work— there is no time to repair them or nurse them along without repair. Manufacturing must therefore be quality-controlled so that close to zero defects regularly prevails. Performance expectations must be met, since there is no room for incorrect assumptions. Advertising and labeling must therefore be truthful and guarantees or warranties must be free from "weasels" that cloak truth in ambiguity and publicize the rules while hiding the exceptions. Recourse must be swift and compensating. Laws for consumer protection must therefore be inclusive, unambiguous, and consistently observed.

Unmarried Women Homemakers

To be unmarried and a homemaker is not a new phenomenon but it is a rapidly growing one. Single-occupant households are increasing their number and discretionary purchasing power. Many of them are presided over by women. Households composed of unmarried couples are also increasing. In these households, women play the same life-styled roles as their married homemaker counterparts. Women who are partners in unmarried households may be indistinguishable in their roles from women in married households. On the other hand, single women who live alone are more likely to resemble homemaker careerists.

Unmarried women who make homes for themselves alone—"singles"—play dual roles: they are the *managers* of each attitude and activity pattern they subscribe to, as well as the managed. They manage themselves and are managed by themselves. This enables them to be usually autonomous in their need-fulfillment. Singles have only one voice to listen to—their own. By contrast, married people have the several voices of husband and family.

Autonomy can lead to caprice in decision making about the purchase of goods and services. Variety of offerings may be demanded in product shape, size, color, and other variable attributes so that personal preference, even whimsy, may be catered to. Convenience products, controlled portions, and multiple-use products meet the needs of singles life-styles. So, paradoxically, do disposables and long-lasting products: Disposables meet the need for managing the singles' environment by preventing clutter and freeing limited storage space; long-lasting products meet the need for sustenance in the absence of frequent shopping expeditions for resupply.

In food products, the unmarried homemaker demands high nutrition. She cannot afford the opportunity loss, even more so the financial cost, of illness "down time." In drugs, self-medication is vital for the same reason. Services that are built into products or that provide timesaving, worksaving benefits are valued even beyond their premium cost because of their perceived premium values: supplying freedom from onerous tasks so that the rewards of freedom to allocate limited time resources can be maximized.

Unmarried homemakers provide a market for fads, for avant-garde trend-setting products, for products that fit their highly mobile activity patterns, and for wide-ranging forms of mobility itself. Psychic transport through innovative experiences as well as physical travel are preferential offerings to people who have no family ties, the ability to apply discretionary income without the need to be called to account, and a strong absence of anxiety about experimenting with new things or of guilt about self-indulgence.

The second type of unmarried homemaker—women who make homes for others as well as themselves, even though their relationships are not formally contractual—are practically indistinguishable in their life-style roles at home from married women homemakers. Their attitude and activity patterns, along with the products and services that provide match-ups for them, are similar to those described in Appendix A. These relationships between product and service needs and the life-style patterns of married women homemaker-careerists and unmarried women homemakers are indicated on the matrix shown in Exhibit 16.

Exhibit 16. Married/Unmarried Homemaker-Careerist life-styled roles and needs

LIFE-STYLED ROLES		PRODUCT AND SERVICE NEEDS
Married Women Homemakers in Their Second Role as Careerists	**1** Home Life-Styles	Similar to Non-Careerist Married Women Homemaker needs, with emphasis on greater convenience from products and more supportive prepackaged services.
	2 Work Life-Styles	a. Business clothes and accessories. b. Psychological stress counseling. c. Training and development education in business management.

Unmarried Women Homemakers	**1** Home Life-Styles
	   Partners
	
	   Singles
		Similar to Married Women Homemakers
		a. Athletic and physical conditioning equipment.
		b. Portion-controlled instant, convenience, and high-nutrition foods.
		c. Twenty-four hour banking services.
		d. Travel services.

	2 Work Life-Styles	Similar to Careerist Married Women Homemakers

Married Women Homemakers

In Exhibit 17 a life-styled marketing opportunity plan is outlined. This plan is designed to enable a developer to structure a vaguely defined area of general interest such as the married woman homemaker market into a workable target for new product generation. As the plan shows, the developer who follows it will be able to take a vague management directive and penetrate a variety of life-styled markets composed of married women homemakers in their various attitudes and activity patterns. He will then have to organize these life-styled markets into a priority rank order which will represent the most profitable allocation of his resources.

The construction of a rank-ordered compendium of life-styled markets which represent the targets for a developer's new product opportunity plan is a formidable task no matter what the nature of the market. For a market composed of married women homemakers, it is especially difficult. Not only are homemakers so extraordinarily diversified in the attitude and activity patterns they manage; the familiar marketing approaches to them have been so scattered and piecemeal and on such an individual product or single need basis for so long that it is a genuine challenge for a developer to organize them as they exist in the homemakers' real world. For these reasons, the problem of life-styling the homemaker market is an excellent example of how an unusually vague area of general interest can be mapped to yield new product opportunities.

The developer's constant perplexity is where to begin. A good rule of thumb is to begin with what is already available. This usually means that the developer pools his own experience, the corroborative experience of his associates, and whatever available secondary data he can get

Exhibit 17. Life-styled marketing opportunity plan.

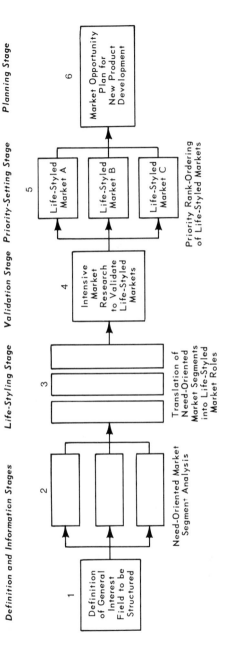

his hands on. The developer never really knows in advance what information will turn out to be grist for his mill. For example, by using a method worked out with John Luther (on behalf of General Foods), a developer beginning to organize the marketing potential of married women homemaker life-styles might start out with a brief list of events that induce significant amounts of change into the average homemaker's life patterns:

Event area 1: Health, illness, and injury
Event area 2: Retirement and death
Event area 3: Marriage, reconciliation, separation, and divorce
Event area 4: Pregnancy and birth
Event area 5: New home acquisition
Event area 6: Vacations
Event area 7: Social activities

The causes of high impact on a homemaker's living style are not life-style roles themselves, but they can be helpful in steering the developer into a thinking groove that will pay off for him in terms of a usable system. Event area 1, for instance, can stimulate the sort of thinking that eventually results in organizing the homemaker's family physician life-style.

A second helpful way for the developer to begin is to set up a minimum number of criteria according to which he will award life-style status to a pattern of homemaking attitudes and activities. Five screening considerations which have been used successfully as criteria by several developers are reproduced here as models.

1. Each life-style must represent a *marketable entity*. That is, it should represent a pattern of attitudes and activities meaningful enough to its practitioners to be rea-

sonably exclusive of other patterns in its key aspects. This criterion attempts to guarantee a consistent, definable market.

2. Each life-style must have needs which are *commercially exploitable*. This criterion attempts to guarantee that a market is being framed for profit-making products and services rather than, say, for philanthropic activities.

3. Each life-style must be *active* and *decision making*. Passive roles, where products and services are imposed on a market or must be accepted without the exercise of preference, should be rejected. This rules out the life-style role of the married woman homemaker as, for example, a hospital or nursing home patient where the marketing opportunity is primarily institutional rather than individual. This criterion attempts to underwrite a marketing approach that can achieve results from individually directed persuasion.

4. Each life-style must be lived out by a middle-income *mass market* or an upper-income *specialty market*. This criterion attempts to ensure the cost-effectiveness of developmental and marketing functions by directing them against populous or affluent targets.

5. As far as possible, each life-style must be based on *repetitive attitude and activity patterns* that have a high rate of turnover in the marketplace and that take place on either a predictably frequent schedule or at least a randomly recurrent basis. This criterion attempts to warrant an active, busy market with a high rate of repeat purchase.

A compendium of married women homemaker lifestyles is presented in Appendix A. Each of the six lifestyle roles described is fleshed out with a "shopping list" of product and service concepts that are compatible with its needs.

A Priority Positioning of Life-Styles
and Their Roles

The compendium of homemaker life-styles shown in Appendix A helps the developer answer the question, Where are the most profitable new product opportunities likely to be found? It does not, however, suggest a rank order for the priority development of opportunities. That is, it does not answer the question, When should each opportunity be exploited?

We have seen how an answer to the question, "When?" is vital to the developer's proper allocation of resources on a first-things-first basis. It is also imperative if the developer wants to be able to serve his markets with new products that can justify a premium pricing policy because they meet the market's major needs.

Creating a priority positioning for life-style roles is only partially objective. To a considerable degree it must always be subjective. The objectivity in the process comes from the market's most urgent needs. These must be allowed to magnetize the developer's priorities. Being objective, they will be essentially similar for all developers. The subjective factors in assigning priorities come from the individual capabilities and objectives of the developer's company. Even though they may be well aware of its existence, top management may not want to press a market's "hot button" if it does not seem to be in keeping with their concept of the company, its goals, or its philosophies. Or management simply may not be able to exploit an opportunity if the required capabilites are in short supply or have a low degree of sophistication. In the final analysis, therefore, every developer's priorities are a mixture of market fact and corporate fact which—in terms of their ultimate outcome—is most often steered in the direction of corporate fact.

Appendix B demonstrates an approach to a priority positioning for six married woman homemaker life-styles. Each priority rating is based on an average of four subsidiary ratings that act as criteria for the developer's screening process:

Corporate Criteria
1. Consonance of a life-style's demand factors with corporate assets and liabilities.
2. Consonance of a life-style's demand factors with corporate financial objectives.

Market Criteria
1. Relevance of a life-style's demand factors to 1980–1990 market needs.
2. Susceptibility of a life-style's demand factors to innovation for 1980–1990 benefits.

Corporate financial objectives come down to the developer from top management. The developer will have to get the substance for the other three criteria for himself. He must be careful not to allow a halo effect to blur his vision of corporate liabilities whose existence, unless brought to consciousness, can prevent successful entry into areas of new interest. A list of corporate assets, as he will discover, comes readily enough. But it is the liabilities which have the power to forestall his success. It is essential that he put them down on paper at the outset of a development program. Otherwise they may show themselves for the first time within the developer's organization or—even worse—in the marketplace once a program has gotten under way.

The developer's screen of market criteria forms a short but succinct test of how well he knows his customer targets. The criterion with respect to market needs requires him to project his knowledge forward into the next decade of developmental time and investment. His projections, of course, will be assumptions, but they can nonetheless be reasonably well founded in the social, economic, political, and technological trends that are visible at any time in a marketplace. The following list contains some of the market needs that may be assumed for packaged-goods consumers in the 1980s.

1. Market needs will become increasingly personalized and humanized, with need segmentation based more and more strictly on the requirements of the individual consumer rather than of consumer groups.
2. Market needs will restlessly seek expression through shorter life-cycled product and service benefits which may remain marketable at peak price points for an average of only two to three years.
3. Market needs will increasingly originate in the attitude and activity patterns of the 1980–1990 decade rather than carrying over traditionally from the lifestyles of preceding decades.
4. Market needs will increasingly originate with two age groups: the 16- to 26-year-old and the 50-plus senior groups.
5. Market needs will increasingly require social benefits to be combined with commercial benefit values in major product and service systems, and will be increasingly intolerant of commercial systems which contribute to social or environmental deficits.
6. Market needs will increasingly demand the synergistic benefits of systems, rather than solo benefits from individual products or services.
7. Market needs will become increasingly permissive of personal indulgence, not in the sense of purchase for the sake of purchase but of use for the sake of oneself and one's own individual version of the quality of life.

8. Market needs will be increasingly directed to reveal the possession of intellectual achievement as sophisticated consumers and emotional energy as social influencers rather than economic affluence.

A second category of market criteria for life-style priorities refers to the innovative susceptibilities of new products or services. To put forth a working list of these criteria, the developer will once again have to make projections on the basis of apparent current trends. Most of these trends, expressed in the following list of apparent susceptibilities to innovation that will be required of consumer packaged goods in the 1980s, will always be well within the framework of common knowledge among developers.

1. Products and services must be susceptible to a high degree of self-styled individualization and a correspondingly lower degree of mass commercialization in appearance and in claims of performance.
2. Products must be susceptible to a high degree of portability and transportability over time and distance, and services must be more universally available and convenient.
3. Products must be susceptible to a high degree of miniaturization, and services must be subject to condensation in speed of delivery or application.
4. Products and services must be susceptible to a high degree of simplification in order to provide the ultimate in convenience with little or no polluting waste.
5. Products and services must be susceptible to iron-clad warranties to document performance claims.
6. Product packaging must be susceptible to recycling if it is disposable or to self-degradable action if it is not recyclable.

7. Products must be susceptible to multiple-purpose use—for example, a hair shampoo which cleans hair and removes dandruff simultaneously, or an aspirin which reduces pain and also tranquilizes.
8. At the same time, paradoxically, other products must be susceptible to highly specific, single-purpose use at the optimal level of effective performance for that category of product.

To give the developer a bird's-eye view of the priorities assigned to all the life-style roles he has structured, it is useful to bring them together within the framework of a matrix such as Exhibit 18. In the exhibit, two of the 21 life-style roles have been awarded a No. 1 priority, four roles have a No. 2 priority, and six more roles have a No. 3 priority. A total of twelve homemaker life-style roles are thus positioned for developmental consideration on a highly urgent basis.

If he chooses to follow a direction which the matrix imparts, the developer may well decide to hedge his bets by adopting an "express track/local track" strategy. This would allow him to commit the lion's share of his resources to the express track by dealing with the homemaker on a priority basis as family physician in her health management role. At the same time, he can begin to develop new products and services on a slower local track for the same homemaker in, for example, a secondary priority role of child trainer. This two-track approach gives him a simultaneous toehold in two high-ranking market areas which contain many potential synergies between them, especially regarding the family physician's relationships with her children. The developer's possibilities are thereby automatically multiplied. Beyond that advantage, he has wisely equipped himself with a fall-back position.

Exhibit 18.   Priority-positioning matrix of homemaker life-style roles.

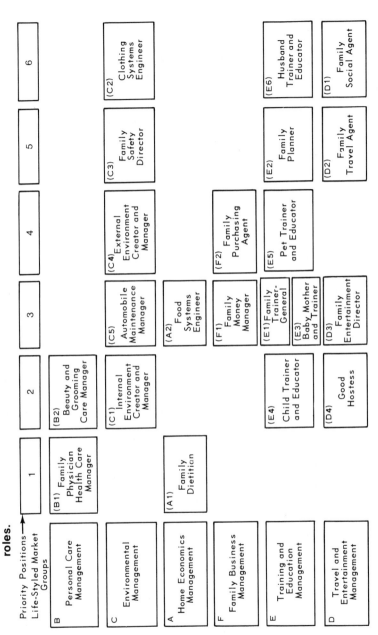

Priority Positions →

Life-Styled Market Groups	1	2	3	4	5	6
B Personal Care Management	(B1) Family Physician Health Care Manager	(B2) Beauty and Grooming Care Manager				
C Environmental Management		(C1) Internal Environment Creator and Manager	(C5) Automobile Maintenance Manager	(C4) External Environment Creator and Manager	(C3) Family Safety Director	(C2) Clothing Systems Engineer
A Home Economics Management	(A1) Family Dietitian		(A2) Food Systems Engineer			
F Family Business Management			(F1) Family Money Manager	(F2) Family Purchasing Agent		
E Training and Education Management		(E4) Child Trainer and Educator	(E1) Family Trainer-General / (E3) Baby, Mother and Trainer	(E5) Pet Trainer and Educator	(E2) Family Planner	(E6) Husband Trainer and Educator
D Travel and Entertainment Management		(D4) Good Hostess	(D3) Family Entertainment Director		(D2) Family Travel Agent	(D1) Family Social Agent

Using a Life-Styled Compendium to Structure
an Attitude and Activity Pattern

It is becoming increasingly fashionable for companies to define the scope of their businesses in broad, often comprehensive terms within which a spectrum of product and service systems can be integrated. This gives top management a welcome flexibility in penetrating many different kinds of businesses. It can also carry with it additional benefits in management's relations with the investment community and with its shareholders and employees, perhaps even conferring a competitive advantage against a more narrowly defined rival. For the new product developer, however, it is invariably a mixed blessing. On the one hand, a broad definition of the corporate business can give the developer considerable latitude in exploring many diverse avenues of innovation. Yet it can make his task exceedingly difficult since a wide choice of directions may result in his ending up with no direction at all.

In line with the growing propensity to spend more discretionary time and income on non-work-related attitude and activity patterns, many businesses have come to define one of their principal areas of concern as the broad field of *leisure*. Industrial manufacturers as well as consumer product marketers either have entered the so-called leisure market or have moved their entire organizations toward the image of a leisure-time producer. Service companies have also joined the leisure bandwagon, especially those in travel and education services. Their developers have had a field day in coming up with self-enjoyment or self-improvement ideas that, for the most part, have been received by their markets as temporary fads rather than as new fashions in higher-quality living. Some developers, reflecting on their experiences with many in-and-out packaged crazes, have borrowed a phrase from the travel business to describe this predictably unsuccessful situation as the if-it's-Tuesday-it-must-be-Belgium syndrome.

Sometimes, when a company gives its mission only the vague characterization of leisure, the developer's work is simplified by the nature of his company's technology. This is often the case when, for example, a home builder extends his technical knowledge from fixed-location homes to mobile homes or when an automobile and truck manufacturer turns to off-the-road vehicles or campers. But more often than not the developer's challenge is an undefined one. Without a technical base that is extendable or even convertible, he may be charged with responsibility to take his company into leisure business opportunities that are totally new to his management and foreign to his own personal experience. At such a point, working from a life-styled market compendium can play a helpful role.

When confronted with such a tenuous concept as the leisure market, the developer's first requirement is to realize that, from his point of view, there is no such entity. Leisure is not a single pattern of attitudes and activities; it is multifaceted. Often it is a complete renunciation of active physical effort or even of psychological involvement for its participants. At other times, its activities can be more vigorous than most forms of work. Many developers have therefore found inspiration in considering leisure not as a market—any more than the youth market is a market—but as an attitude and activity pattern that is the natural accompaniment of several life-styles.

One illustration of a life-style which can offer leisure product or service opportunities is style D in Appendix A, the homemaker's roles in travel and entertainment management. Another of the styles which contains opportunities to commercialize leisure is life-style C, that of environmental management in both its internal and its external manifestations.

A developer who chooses to explore leisure opportunities which may be generated by the married woman homemaker's life-style role as an environmental manager has two options. He can concentrate on the attitudes and activities generated by the homemaker's management of her external environments where huge numbers of potential opportunities exist. Or he can try to zero in on the far tighter frame of internal environment creation and management. Fewer obvious product or service opportunities are apparent in the internal environment. As a matter of fact, the very context of the home's interior design works against the homemaker's participation in many commercializable patterns of leisure.

There are several reasons why this is so. For one, the home is the homemaker's working environment and, as her title makes clear, she is the manager there. By her attitudes and activities as family dietitian, family physician, and all her other life-style roles, she converts what would otherwise be only an architectural environment into an operational home. Few homemakers therefore design their homes for leisure—on the whole, homes are oriented for work management. Psychologically as well as architecturally, the home is far more effective as a commissary, dormitory, and lavatory than as a focal point for leisure.

A second factor that limits leisure opportunities in and around the home is that leisure patterns connote a change from work patterns. This may be their greatest attraction. It is difficult to get away from the household working environment in most homes, and even more unlikely that its intrusions can be entirely shut out or compensated for. For this very reason alone, the patterns involved in the homemaker's life-style role as an environmental manager vironment are frequently so much easier for the developer to serve.

There is a third factor, too: In-home leisure is far more passive than active, or at least far more reactive than active. Killing time, resting and relaxing, and daydreaming are almost universally among the most prevalent attitude and activity patterns associated with leisure in the home's internal environment. These patterns of vicarious participation and guiltless observation fit the dormitory role of the home. They also help explain the existence of television as a universal medium, since television not only provides leisure rewards that can be simply reacted to but it also permits, and perhaps encourages, simultaneous resting and relaxing, daydreaming, or even sleep, which is the ultimate in leisure inactivity. These reactive or passive patterns, which dominate home leisure, are in every case difficult and in many cases impossible to commercialize.

Despite these restrictions of the developer's creativity, he can nonetheless use life-styling to get inside the homemaker's internal management roles and search out new product or service ideas for her acceptance. In Exhibit 19, which shows how one approach to the problem can be made, the developer has taken the homemaker's internal management role of cottage craftsman as his exploratory target. Before making the exhibit, he has previously divided the role into four possible patterns of attitudes and activities, two of which demand initiative on the part of the homemaker and another two which ask only that she respond:

1. *Active-competitive patterns*, in which the home-maker actively confronts the challenge of performing against norms or face to face against other chal-

Exhibit 19. **Life-styled marketing opportunities based on indoor leisure patterns of women homemakers in their role as cottage craftspeople.**

ACTIVE-COMPETITIVE ATTITUDES AND ACTIVITIES	
Alone	*In Group*
Sewing	Sewing clubs
Weaving	
Ceramics	Ceramics clubs
Gardening	Garden clubs and seed business
Card and board games	Card and board game clubs
Drawing and painting	Drawing and painting clubs and correspondence courses
Writing	Writing correspondence courses
Sculpting	
Music making	Music correspondence courses
Photography	Camera clubs and photography correspondence courses
Home decorating	Home decoration courses

lengers in real or game situations. Arts, crafts, gymnastics, and athletics are examples of active-competitive leisure patterns.

2. *Active-cooperative patterns,* in which the homemaker coordinates her attitudes and activities in face-to-face situations with other people or indirectly through communications media. Many social activities, hostessing, and some gymnastics are examples of active-cooperative leisure patterns.

3. *Reactive-competitive patterns,* in which the homemaker responds competitively to the confrontations of others either in face-to-face situations or indirectly through communications media. Viewing sports con-

tests on television is an example of a reactive-competitive leisure pattern.

4. *Reactive-cooperative patterns,* in which the home-maker responds cooperatively to the attitudes and activities of others, either in face-to-face situations or indirectly through communications media. Many social activities, reading for pleasure, and most television viewing of nonsports programs are examples of reactive-cooperative leisure patterns.

Because it is a role which places a premium on initiative, the developer has found that the homemaker's cottage craftsman role fits into the active-competitive patterns. In it, the homemaker is competing against norms of perfected performance which are inherent in every craft as well as the achievments of others who have accepted a similar challenge and whose accomplishments may invite comparison. Within the cottage craftsman role, the developer has been able to identify 11 potentially commercializable leisure patterns. (See Exhibit 19.) Some of them are solitary patterns with which each individual homemaker can become involved. Others lend themselves to group activity, creating a common focal point around which many homemakers may be able to rally in club form.

A similar procedure has allowed the developer to compile the six patterns whose attitudes and activities are expressed by homemakers in another of their internal environment roles, that of the equity-building collector. In this role, the homemaker is involved in the collection and management of possessions whose accumulation can create an equity for the household. In Exhibit 20, the developer has recorded his estimate of the potentially most marketable patterns of leisure collection. For this role, as well as for the role of cottage craftsman, the developer can

Exhibit 20. **Life-styled marketing opportunities based on indoor leisure patterns of women homemakers in their role as equity-building collectors.**

ACTIVE-COMPETITIVE ATTITUDES AND ACTIVITIES	
Alone	*In Group*
Money accumulating and stock market playing	Investment clubs
Art collecting	Art collecting clubs
Shell collecting	Shell collecting clubs
Antique collecting	Antique collecting clubs
Book collecting	Book-of-the-Month and other book collecting clubs

then select for further study the patterns that best meet commercial criteria (such as the following) which help isolate the high-priority opportunities:

1. The pattern is engaged in by individuals acting in groups as well as alone. If groups do not normally exist, they can be readily stimulated.
2. The pattern has potential involvement for more than the homemaker herself in that it will include the creation of useful or admirable outputs for the concern of some or all members of her family.
3. The pattern is extensive by virtue of its regular occurrence throughout the year.
4. The pattern is intensive by virtue of its regular occurence at least once each week.
5. The pattern is accommodating by virtue of its ease of occurrence either in daytime or in nightime.

These criteria are an attempt to help the developer set up a screen which will pass only the opportunity areas that have mass marketing prospects because of their importance to a life-style role's attitude and activity patterns. When these areas have been mapped, they are ready for sifting through a second set of criteria which set forth corporate objectives and preferences. Opportunities which meet these twin sets of standards must then be assigned priorities. In the preceding chapters we have seen that this process is the basis for the developer's commitments. In Chapter 5 we will see another use for the developer's priority mix of life-styled opportunities. If he and his management are serious about seizing the concept of a market and setting about to become its preemptive supplier, he should begin to affect the corporate divisional structure so it can serve it. This way of bringing life-styling directly into the company framework from out in the field is an innovative trend that, for its practitioners, is making life-styled marketing central to the functioning of their businesses.

5

Life-Styled Markets as the Basis for Corporate Organization

Most companies have been put together in the traditional manner of working from the inside out—that is, moving progressively outward from a central processing technology into market commercialization. Each of the major departments and divisions of these companies owes its existence to the technical process which acts as its source of supply. In a packaging manufacturer, for example, there is a metals division which makes rigid containers that are dependent on basic metal-bending and sealing techniques. There is also a plastics division that makes flexible containers which depend on extrusion techniques. This type of organizational structure makes it appear irrelevant that the same decision maker may be the customer for the output of both divisions, or that there may be synergistic values in their combined marketing. Similarly, in a food manufacturer, there are a frozen foods division, a powdered foods division, and a compressed foods division. Here again, the same decision makers—the supermarket retailer and the married woman homemaker—may be customers for the products of all three divisions. But from the point of view of corporate organization, these facts seem unrecognized or immaterial.

Companies organized from the inside out tend to have an unusually difficult time with their new product development and marketing. Living so close to their technologies, they often allow themselves to become remote from their markets. The more enterprising among them realize their remoteness and try to utilize salesforce fact-gathering or customer market research to compensate for it. But it is the act of life-styling their markets that reveals how much the inner world of their business is actually an assumptive world—that is, a world based on assumptions of what their customers "must want" and "will buy." Through the life-styling process, many internal standards of "what will sell" and technical standards of product or process control can also be seen to be the artificial conveniences they really are. In a large number of cases, life-styling spotlights them as being widely different from the standards of acceptance control practiced by a market. More than one development manager has come to this reluctant conclusion: "What we make here so carefully and call the best may be judged to be the least when we take it before our market; our cherished criteria for quality may be the market's criteria for mediocrity or simply overpriced overengineering."

Being within specifications inside a company and being outside specifications in the real world of a marketplace is common. If the past generation of new product management has left any lasting impressions at all in the minds of today's managers, it should be clear that market orientation is the exception rather than the rule in business and will probably remain so for at least one reason: Whereas product orientation is built into a business by its very nature, market orientation must be consciously imposed on a business as a well-studied afterthought. Until the real-world needs of its markets are internalized by a business, they will tend to remain external to it and, by definition, foreign.

It is becoming apparent to companies whose developers are life-styling their markets that one way to internalize their customers' real worlds in the organizational structure of the business is to reconstruct the business backward— that is, from the outside in. This places a life-styled group of customers as the organizational focal point of a business. Their life patterns then become the central process which naturally divides the company into its divisions and departments, dictates the technological capabilities that are to be required, and assigns developmental priorities to its new product creation. When a market is centralized in this way as the source of a business, the organizational style that results is becoming known by a new name, *marketcentric.*

Exhibit 21 illustrates a marketcentric structure for the feminine hygiene company discussed in Chapter 3. In its new form, a parent holding company in the general personal care business has been organized around two basic processing technologies: the company's traditional cellulose science and an acquired pharmaceutical capability. The pharmaceutical technology contributes to ethical drug production for five of the eight markets built around lifestyles. The cellulose processes serve all eight life-styled markets with disposable apparel, accessories, and application materials for many of the ethical products. Each of the newly styled markets is the source of a discrete business for the company whose demand pressures have caused the addition of a pharmaceutical capability in the first place and its subsequent new product developments thereafter.

Such a marketcentric organization can be divided into

Exhibit 21. The marketcentric reorganization of a feminine hygiene company.

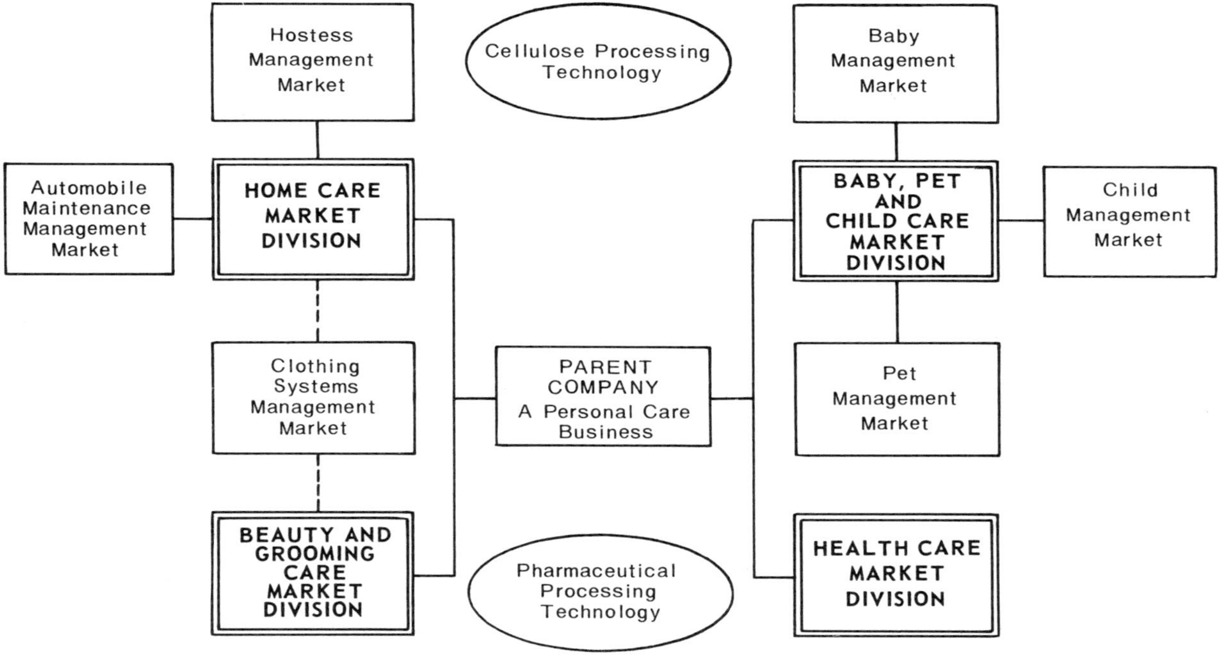

the four major operating units shown in Exhibit 21, each of which is a profit-centered business entity:

1. A health care market division, incorporating the company's health care businesses that serve the family physician life-style role.
2. A beauty and grooming care market division that also includes the clothing care market.
3. A baby, pet, and child care market division.
4. A home care market division that includes hostess management and automobile maintenance management.

Highlights of a Marketcentric Organization

The marketcentric form of organization is distinguished by three features:

1. A market, rather than a product line or a processing technology, is positioned as the focal point of each major business. Each market is defined in life-style terms which reflect its chief needs. This represents a true market-centering of a business. A market, considered as a need group, is treated as the cause of each business. In turn, the business assigns itself the role of acting as its market's primary need-seeking and need-serving group. Structurally as well as conceptually, a market-centered business does not have to learn market orientation—customer-centering is born within it and will be native to it.

2. Each market on which a business is profit-centered is administered by a *business manager*. Unlike a product or brand manager, or even most market managers, the business manager is a corporate entrepreneur. His responsibility is to maximize the profit contributed to his company from doing business with his market. The scope

and diversity of the business he does is limited only by the definition of his market's life-style, not by the synthetic limitations that might otherwise be imposed on him by the boundaries of his company's traditional technology, product lines, or sales and distribution channels.

3. Top management in a marketcentric organization becomes a holding company. It operates as a council of portfolio managers who centralize policy-making and investment strategies for their decentralized, business-managed profit centers. Their prime concern is to manage a balanced portfolio of profitable businesses where no single investment accounts for more than 50 percent of total corporate profit, or at least not for long.

A Business of Market-Oriented Businesses

A marketcentric company can be a business composed of a few businesses or many. Although it is most likely to accommodate the problems and opportunities of medium-size and large multimarket manufacturers, any diversified company can organize profitably along marketcentric lines. All that is required, essentially, is that its management believe in running a business that is a union of businesses: unified at the top by a capital-management holding team yet varied in terms of the life-styled markets that are served, the product and service systems that are marketed to them, and the manufacturing materials and technical processes that are employed.

By expanding and diversifying from within, developers in marketcentric companies are in an excellent position to take advantage of the multiple profit opportunities their business managers enjoy. All the needs of a given market's life-style, not just those benefiting from current corporate technological capabilities, can be considered fair game for a marketcentric company's growth. Because its businesses are not financially interlocked, nor are its business managers operationally dependent on one another, a marketcentric company can expand into a variety of new life-styled businesses serving the same established markets whose needs are well known from experience. This, as we have learned, is a relatively safe kind of growth. By constantly asking the key question, "What other life-style roles are meaningful to these same markets we know so well, and how can we serve them preemptively?" a marketcentric company can continue to move into new product development directly from its existing corporate strength. Accordingly, there need be only two basic rules to govern its new product growth: If it pays, consider getting into it; if it doesn't pay, stay out.

This two-way flexibility comes directly from life-styling a market and then centering the construction of a business around it. Not only can such a market be served *intensively*. When growth and a broadening of the profit base become desirable, the same market can be served more *extensively* by searching out the needs of its other life-style roles and centering the development of new product systems around one or more of them. The ideal objective of the marketcentric process can thus be defined as serving the greatest number of interrelated needs of each market segment where the company's business is importantly committed and from which it earns its principal revenues. It is worthwhile to contrast this approach with the "full line" philosophy of process-oriented manufacturers that tend to offer *something* for everybody. The marketcentric company's stance is to offer *everything* profitable that relates to the same life-style. While it may eventually become product- and service-extensive, it will have grown by being market-intensive in the management of each of its individual marketcentric segments.

The optimal time to market-center a business is at its inception, when the market's needs that it is being organized to serve can be incorporated directly into the company charter. Businesses already under way will have to recharter themselves if their organization is to become marketcentric. This means that they will have to rethink and react on an "as if" basis—as if they were starting out in business today and gearing themselves to operate in the most cost-effective manner.

As each company works out its individual reconciliation with the marketcentric organizational structure, it can at the very least be assured that whatever progress it makes in the direction of increased market orientation is all to the good. Even the start-up effort to market-center itself ought to pay early dividends in new product successes, unlike many other types of corporate reorganization in which the major benefits are achievable only at the tail end of the process. Where a company's new product growth goes from there, and how swiftly, may be a good test of its adaptation to doing business in the last quarter of the twentieth century.

Appendix A

Compendium of Married Woman Homemaker Life-Styles

Summary

Life-Style A: Home Economics Management
    A1. Family dietitian
    A2. Food systems engineer
Life-Style B: Personal Care Management
    B1. Health care manager
    B2. Beauty and grooming care manager
Life-Style C: Environmental Management
    C1. Internal environment creator and manager
    C2. Clothing systems engineer
    C3. Family safety director
    C4. External environment creator and manager
    C5. Automobile maintenance manager
Life-Style D: Travel and Entertainment Management
    D1. Family social agent
    D2. Family travel agent
    D3. Family entertainment director
    D4. Good hostess

Life-Style E: Training and Education Management
        E1. Family trainer-general
        E2. Family planner
        E3. Baby mother and trainer
        E4. Child trainer and educator
        E5. Pet trainer and educator
        E6. Husband trainer and educator
Life-Style F: Family Business Management
        F1. Family money manager
        F2. Family purchasing agent

Life-Style A
Home Economics Management

A1. The married woman homemaker in her life-style role as family dietitian.

The middle majority homemaker, age 19 to 49, in her roles as food selector and meal balancer, daily menu planner, and culinary artisan and food stylist.

Product and service system categories compatible with this role include foods, functional foods, and food analogs; meal planning and menu planning consultation services; recipe services; food-styling consultation and education services; fast-food franchise services; computerized food ordering and delivery services; and televised or franchised cooking schools.

A2. The married woman homemaker in her life-style role as food systems engineer.

The middle majority homemaker, age 19 to 49, in her roles as skilled operator of food storage, cooking, serving, and disposal systems; meal planning and menu rationalizing systems; and utensil cleaning, maintenance, and storage systems.

Product and service system categories compatible with this role include household appliance systems; appliance layout consultation services; appliance operation consultation services; appliance maintenance and repair services; service contract consultation service or books; disposable utensil product lines; detergents and ultrasonic cleaning systems; and appliance rental services.

Life-Style B
Personal Care Management

B1. The married woman homemaker in her life-style role as personal health care manager.

The middle majority homemaker, age 19 to 59, in her roles as family physician and nurse, family physical-health and mental-health educator.

Product and service system categories compatible with this role include internally and externally applied drugs, health foods, and functional foods; computerized health care and consultation services; self-diagnostic kits; clinics and care centers; disposable products; health education services and media; and feminine hygiene products and services.

B2. The married woman homemaker in her life-style role as personal beauty and grooming care manager.

The middle majority homemaker, age 19 to 59, in her roles as socially attractive woman in public situations and seductively attractive wife or lover in private situations.

Product and service system categories compatible with this role include internal beauty care products such as beauty foods and beauty drugs; external beauty care products such as hair, face, and body cosmetics, fashionable apparel and beauty care services such as beauty consultation, product prescription services, computerized complexion analysis, self-styling systems of beauty care, and shopping services of various kinds.

Life-Style C
Environmental Management

C1. The married woman homemaker in her life-style role as internal environment creator and manager.

The middle majority homemaker, age 19 to 59, in her roles as interior decorator and mood stylist for the home; cottage craftsman; equity-building collector; communications systems manager; home repairman and service contract negotiator with external repair and manufacturing services; family maid and sanitary engineer.

Product and service system categories compatible with this role include interior decoration consultation services and media; home repair kits and manuals; home furnishings for sale or rent; in-home communications systems; home repair contractual and insurance services; modular home-study centers; maid rental services; bathroom equipment and fixtures; saunas; household insurance services; and service contract consultation services.

C2. The married woman homemaker in her life-style role as clothing systems engineer.

The middle majority homemaker, age 19 to 49, in her roles as skilled operator of clothes cleaning, drying, pressing, and maintenance systems.

Product and service system categories compatible with this role include appliance systems; appliance consultation, maintenance, and repair services; service contract consultation services; appliance rental services; appliance layout consultation services; detergents and ultrasonic cleaning systems; sewing and mending systems; and protective anticrease, antiwrinkle, and antistain products.

C3. The married woman homemaker in her life-style role as family safety director.

The middle majority homemaker, age 19 to 49, in her roles as family policeman, family fireman, family planner, and manager of emergency stores and services.

Product and service system categories compatible with this role include home security devices and protective equipment; home fire-alarm and fire-fighting equipment and instruction; individual self-protection education and tools; emergency foodstuffs; and safety and protective equipment rental and services.

C4. The married woman homemaker in her life-style role as external environment creator and manager.

The middle majority homemaker, age 19 to 59, in her roles as architect and homebuilder; gardener and landscaper; outdoor living planner; general property-value manager; and service contract negotiator with external repair and manufacturing services.

Product and service system categories compatible with this role include home rental or purchasing consultation services; home improvement products and services; home repair kits and manuals; property-value maintenance instruction and information services; gardening tools, seeds, and planning services; synthetic lawns and other home decoration products and services; landscape rental services; disposable landscaping; landscape insurance; children's exercise equipment; pools and solaria; and service contract consultation.

C5. The married woman homemaker in her life-style role as automobile maintenance manager.

The middle majority homemaker, age 19 to 49, in her roles as family chauffeur, automobile repair and maintenance manager, and correspondent with external automobile repair and maintenance services.

Product and service system categories compatible with this role include automobile driving instruction schools and information services; periodic computerized automobile maintenance and repair services; service contract and repair estimate consultation services; and automobile repair diagnostic clinics.

Life-Style D
Travel and Entertainment Management

D1. The married woman homemaker in her life-style role as family social agent.

The middle majority homemaker, age 19 to 49, in her roles as external representative of the family in social, civic, and other community affairs.

Product and service system categories compatible with this role include self-styling consultation and educational services in dress, makeup, diction, speechmaking, and social poise; civic affairs consulation, group organization, and planning services; and club entertainment planning services.

D2. The married woman homemaker in her life-style role as family travel agent.

The middle majority homemaker, age 19 to 59, in her roles as vacation selector and planner.

Product and service system categories compatible with this role include vacation-styling services; vacation packs of portable foods, drugs, and cosmetics; disposable vacation apparel and accessories; and computerized vacation planning services.

D3. The married woman homemaker in her life-style role as family entertainment director.

The middle majority homemaker, age 19 to 49, in her roles as amusement selector and censor, leisure-time planner, toy and game buyer, arts and crafts hobbyist and buyer, and family athletic director.

Product and service system categories compatible with this role include leisure time planning services; toy, game, and craft products; athletic equipment and instruction services; athletics-oriented cosmetics and quick-energy foods; first-aid equipment and preventive or remedial products such as suntan lotions and sprays or pills, aerosol bandages, and hot and cold packs; picnic and camping equipment; outdoor and backyard living equipment; sporting clubs and groups; country clubs; boats; and skiing-related manufacturing and rental services.

D4. The married woman homemaker in her life-style role as good hostess.

The middle majority homemaker, age 19 to 59, in her roles as official greeter of friends, neighbors, and relatives; and party planner and party giver within the boundaries of the home.

Product and service system categories compatible with this role include complete hostess rental services, party provisioning, and sanitation; disposable apparel, accessories, furnishings, and appurtenances; party foods, snacks, and shelf-stable "just-in-case" foods and beverages; and party planning service.

Life Style E
Training and Education Management

E1. The married woman homemaker in her life-style role as family trainer-general.

The middle majority homemaker, age 19 to 49, in her roles as family taste arbiter and style setter; family moralist and values manager; religious high-priestess; and family schedule maker and rule recorder.

Product and services system categories compatible with this role include services; time-and-attention allocation and budgeting guides; and family values consultation services.

E2. The married woman homemaker in her life-style role as family planner.

The middle majority homemaker, age 19 to 49, in her role as conception controller and family planner.

Product and service system categories compatible with this role include contraceptive products and instructional services; related menstrual products and instructional services; family planning consultation services and family planning insurance.

E3. The married woman homemaker in her life-style role as mother.

The middle majority homemaker, age 19 to 39, in her roles as entertainer and teacher of babies.

Product and service system categories compatible with this role include baby-care instruction and education books, films, classes, and other consultation services; toys and games; baby accessories, apparel, and disposables; and reward-type foods.

E4. The married woman homemaker in her life-style role as child trainer and educator.

The middle majority homemaker, age 19 to 49, in her roles as child entertainer and teacher.

Product and service system categories compatible with this role include child-care instruction and education books, films, classes, and other consultation services; children's toys, games, and crafts; children's preschool educational services and tools; children's accessories, apparel, and equipment for school; disposable training and education aids; child health insurance; and children's college enrollment insurance.

E5. The married woman homemaker in her life-style role as pet trainer and educator.

The middle majority homemaker, age 19 to 49, in her roles as animal and bird purchaser, feeder, teacher, entertainer, and health manager.

Product and service system categories compatible with this role include franchised kennels and aviaries; pet foods; pet accessories, disposable apparel, and toys; pet-care instruction services; pet health insurance; and pet-care and -maintenance services.

E6. The married woman homemaker in her life-style role as husband trainer and educator.

The middle majority homemaker, age 19 to 49, in her roles as husband career guide and advancer.

Product and service system categories compatible with this role include books, films, classes, and other educational services offering instruction in life-styling for the wife–husband team; role consultation and computerized information services on role relationships; and books, films, classes, and other information services for housewives to educate them on their husbands' career needs and opportunities for them to help with their husbands' advancement.

Life-Style F
Family Business Management

F1. The married woman homemaker in her life-style role as family money manager.

The middle majority homemaker, age 19 to 59, in her roles as family treasurer and credit manager; family accountant and budgeter; and family estate executor.

Product and service system categories compatible with this role include household budget planning educational services and computerized budget-keeping services; investment advisory services; and food-budget planning guides.

F2. The married woman homemaker in her life-style role as family purchasing agent.

The middle majority homemaker, age 19 to 49, in her roles as comparison shopper, buyer, and order taker within the family.

Product and service system categories compatible with this role include shopping consultation services; buyer education classes, books, films, and television programs; product comparison services; labeling and packaging guides for smart shopping; and gift suggestion and purchasing services.

Appendix B

Priority Positioning of Married Woman Homemaker Life-Styles in the 1980-1990 Decade

Summary

Priority #1: Personal Care Management
Priority #2: Environmental Management
Priority #3: Home Economics Management
Priority #4: Family Business Management
Priority #5: Training and Education Management
Priority #6: Travel and Entertainment Management

Priority #1: Personal Care Management

Health care manager

Beauty and grooming care manager

*Supportive Sociotechnological Opportunities
and Preclusive Risks*

Health care opportunities. Increasing public acceptance of health care as a natural right, and a resultant increase in degree and level of public and private involvement in health care and education. Inadequacy and cost-ineffectiveness of existing professional care system will require deemphasis of MD and hospital as care centers and will encourage deprofessionalization of care to the in-home level. New emphasis on early diagnosis, prevention, and therapy rather than remedial treatment or curative products and services. Growing acceptance of drug values of foods. Increased awareness of health values of psychic experiences.

Health care risks. Governmental and professional medical community resistance to "paramedicalization," deprofessionalization, and other key aspects of therapeutic self-diagnosis and commercially sponsored therapy. High educational input required with both homemaker and professional communities.

Beauty and grooming care opportunities. Multiplied opportunities arising from increasing social correlation of health and beauty, leading to systems potential between foods and cosmetics, beauty and exercise or entertainment, beauty and fashionable apparel and accessories, and the union of psychic and physical health. Emphasis on self-styled care systems which stress individualized beauty. Involvement of the entire family (rather than just the woman) in beauty and grooming. Involvement of the entire body in beauty and grooming, with beauty conceived of as the body's outermost garment of clothing.

Beauty care risks. Saturation of existing distribution systems and difficulty in establishing profitable alternatives. Difficulties of marketing coordinated product systems in a traditionally individual-item business. Increasing governmental sensitivities to drug implications of health-oriented cosmetics. Limiting effects of stepped-up consumerism on beauty care advertising and promotional positioning. Beauty business is style-intensive, stressing high risk over short, faddish product life cycles for potential high reward.

Comments. Health care management is a genuinely new business which has never existed before. As such, it offers attractive opportunities across a wide variety of corporate technological bases. No company has a preemptive manufacturing or marketing foundation. The so-called health care industry, which is really a sick care industry, may enjoy some slight initial advantage, especially in terms of acceptance by the professional medical community. But to the extent that sick care companies are treatment-oriented instead of prevention-oriented, and to the degree that health care can become deprofessionalized and popularized, this advantage may be only transient. Because of its meaningfulness to the total population, and because of its freshness as a market, the health care field will undoubtedly be attractive to investment during the 1980s and could become the nation's largest industry well within that time.

Priority #2: Environmental Management

> Internal environment creator and manager
> Clothing systems engineer
> Family safety director
> External environment creator and manager
> Automobile maintenance manager

Supportive Sociotechnological Opportunities and Preclusive Risks

Internal environment opportunities. Greater interest in environmental coordination of furnishings, appliances, and accessories by means of systems. Increasing acceptance by women of "man of the house" role, opening new decision-making opportunities and product options. Increasing acceptance of rental as opposed to purchase options and of disposable options as opposed to permanent possession. New concepts and materials proliferation, including plastics and other synthetics, inflatables, foldables, storables, multiple-purpose units, and portables. Greater needs for emergency, security, and safety products and services in the face of increasing crime and social unrest. Increased desire for privacy and individualization of internal environment. Heightened acceptance of interior environment as education–entertainment–information center for family. Potential correlation with food systems engineering to create programmed home cooking center as environmental focal point. Potential correlation of home business management center with family business management life-style role of money handling.

Internal environment risks. Rapid product obsolescence. Increasing competition from out-of-home discretionary investments. Dependence on appliance-service orientation and appliance-type distribution system. Involvement is complicated by interrelationships between electronics technology, plumbing, heating, electricity, fixtures, home construction codes, and labor union restrictions.

External environment opportunities. Greater acceptance of external environment as extension of indoors (the lawn as carpeting, the auto as a portable room). Increasing acceptance of rental as opposed to purchase options and of disposable options as opposed to permanent possession. New concepts and new materials, including plastics and other synthetics, foldables and storables, prefabricated and modular units. Range of external environment expanded by means of house trailers and houseboats (which make a second homesite available almost anywhere), ski houses, summer houses, and other types of second homes. Greater needs for property value insurance and security and safety products and services because of increasing crime and social unrest. Correlations with training, education, travel, and entertainment.

External environment risks. Rapid product obsolescence. External environmental deterioration and resulting governmental regulation may limit extension and discourage involvement or investment.

Comments. Environmental management, both internal and external, is not a truly new business even though it may seem to be. Instead, it is largely a new systematization of many heretofore individual businesses which have recently positioned themselves in alliance with each other. Time-space and geographical space are now equally regarded as environments, and there can be a high degree of potential profitability in seeking to fill them since each is more encompassing than ever before. Discretionary time-space for work, education, and leisure is increasing and probably will continue to increase throughout the decade of the 1980s. Commercial options ought to be able to increase to fill its needs. The range of the individual in utilizing geographical space is virtually unlimited for commercialization by travel and entertainment benefits. Opportunities here will undoubtedly multiply as well. There is also the opportunity to commercialize many benefits for the use of intellectual space, which is the object of training and educational life-style roles. Use of these several environments may well become a key criterion of the quality of life being lived by each individual, as well as a standard of the public value of his contributions. Thus the social concern of environmental use, as well as personal concern, will probably continue to be a paramount standard in the marketplace.

Priority #3: Home Economics Management

Family dietitian
Food systems engineer

Supportive Sociotechnological Opportunities and Preclusive Risks

Opportunities. New emphasis on nutrition, functional and health foods, natural foods, and food purity. Technical feasibility of computerized meal planning, supermarket-showroom and telephone food ordering and delivery systems. Increasing technical feasibility and social acceptance of food analogs. Acceptance of special-purpose foods such as body-growth foods, mind-keening foods, beauty foods, age-retarding and life-extending foods. Disposable food cooking, serving, and storing systems.

Individualized servings and portion-calorie-controlled foods. Acceptance of multiple light meal-ettes to replace traditional three sit-down square meals per day.

Risks. Shorter life cycles for food products. Prospects for advertising media and supermarket distribution saturation in the face of new food product proliferation. Speculative positioning stance toward food analogs by regulatory and distribution agencies as imitations, substitutes, or new foods. Potentially lessening role emphasis of food-oriented attitudes and activities in the face of women's new freedoms and outside concerns.

Comments. Although the regularity of the homemaker's need to feed and nourish her family as home economics manager will probably not decrease perceptibly during the 1980s, the relative importance of the homemaker's role as foodmaker may decline in her overall role-mix. The very opportunities which make home economics management profitably rewarding may accelerate the lessening of its opportunity. First, as food-related attitudes and activities become more and more convenient, homemaker involvement may diminish. Even benign conspiracies such as "adding the egg" may no longer suffice to simulate participation. Second, the automation of food ordering, menu planning, and payment will probably reduce the onerous and truly time-consuming aspects of some of the most typical home economics processes. Third, the 1980s generation of homemakers may well rebel against kitchen-centered life-styles and food orientation in favor of more external, more liberated, and more self-expressive roles.

For these reasons, home economics management may well be a role in downward transition during the 1980s. The greatest risk lies in *not* pioneering. Two innovative directions seem most promising of reward. One is the functionalization of foods, emphasizing their nutrition and health orientation as if they were delicious drugs; the second is the acknowledgment of the net result of technological developments in food distribution, shopping, and purchase planning, along with an increasing homemaker need for convenience and preplanning and a rising attitude of concern toward the family dietitian role.

Priority *#4:* Family Business Management
Family money manager
Family purchasing agent

Supportive Sociotechnological Opportunities and Preclusive Risks

Opportunities. Increasing feasibility of in-home access to computerized information and data processing services in family business management as a convenience item. Heightened potential of cashless society aspects occurring during the decade of the 1980s. Greater need to systematize multiple family investment options. Growing need for multiple hedges against enduring inflationary dollar erosion. Inexperienced affluence leads to needs for money management advisory and planning services. Rise of interest in consumerism leads to need for increased purchase, label, and packaging information services. Enduring discrepancy between ages of death of husband and wife may lead to need for generalized estate planning services for homemakers. Opportunity to integrate with family dietitian life-style and establish purchasing-agent-for-food money management services.

Risks. High educational investment may be required to transform an individualistic, cottage-industry activity into an acceptable commercial function. Potentially high resistance to invasion of fiscal privacy by perceived "Big Brother" image of business management information collection and disbursement services. Technologically intensive and service-intensive business.

Comments. Family business management is an area of profit potential whose relatively low priority ought not to obscure its potential through the 1980s. Taken at its fullest, family business management is a processing business based on computerized data manipulation as its fundamental process. The process is essentially resolved into an investment planning service, with the word "investment" used in its broadest possible context to include all allocations of family economic resources. In this sense, family business management will become more important as affluence increases investment options and inflation reduces the prospective value of each decision.

Priority #5: Training and Education Management

Family trainer-general
Family planner
Baby mother and trainer
Child trainer and educator
Pet trainer and educator
Husband trainer and educator

A Supportive Sociotechnological Opportunities and Preclusive Risks

Opportunities. Heightened interest in a wide range of educational activities through in-home and outside-home services: in-home multimedia audiovisual learning systems, study centers, and teaching machines, as well as outside computerized libraries and local learning centers. Greater availability of correspondence study programs and courses in a broad spectrum of subject areas. Educational emphasis placed on vacations, leisure-time activities, social activities, and work, and on self-adjustment, self-selection of knowledge areas, and individual growth. Growing acceptance of behavioral sensitivity training and psychosocial acculturation as normal parts of general education. Greater acceptance of educational toys, games, crafts, and foods. Correlations with travel, entertainment, and all other life-styles.

Risks. Unstable market over the short term because of inevitable shakeout and consolidation of currently overpopulated knowledge industry. Failure of technology to regularize second-generation teaching machine performance. Critical sellers' market in educational software.

Comments. Training and educational management is actually two roles with the same name. First, it is a role in itself, with the homemaker acting in ways that develop the intellectual and behavioral capabilities of the family as a group and of its individual members. Second, it is an implicit component of every other life-style role which the homemaker plays. As a role itself, training and education has so far been an unstable industry—its hardware capability has eclipsed its software content. The language of systems has been used to disguise the absence of a true systematization in either manufacturing or marketing. On the basis of this background, it is difficult to assess the next decade of development of the education business or so-called knowledge industry. It is easier to foresee an opportunity of clearer magnitude for training and education management activities as adjuncts to all the other major life roles. This suggests that an information module be considered an integral characteristic of every major product and service system. It also encourages the wisdom of conceiving of information sources as profit-making corporate media, instead of regarding only products as media, and establishing those information media as the major creators of market preference for the products which may, in a subordinate or supplementary role, accompany them.

Priority #6: Travel and Entertainment Management

> Family social agent
> Family travel agent
> Family entertainment director
> Good hostess

Supportive Sociotechnological Opportunities and Preclusive Risks

Opportunities. Greater mobility and sense of worldliness predispose to wide-ranging travel acceptance. Travel is becoming more informal and periodic and is taking on many attributes of an impulse purchase. Traditional annual vacation is fractionalizing into multiple "vacation-ettes." Heightened acceptance of rental and disposable vacation products and accessories. Growing guest diversity of in-home entertainment gatherings, including multiracial and multi-life-style gatherings. Greater emphasis on cause-oriented socializing and entertainment. More leisure-time and discretionary options for its use through travel and entertainment, leading to enhanced equipment and educational opportunities for athletic, hobby, camping, and allied activities. Increasing acceptance of rent-a-party services. Correlations with snack and disposables development, training and education and family business management life-styles.

Risks. Domestic and international unrest may preclude travel interest and opportunities. Environmental deterioration may also act as discouraging or limiting factor.

Comments. Travel and entertainment will increasingly become intertwined throughout the 1980s. As the commercialization of leisure proceeds, travel will become more convenient, affordable, and acceptable, and will undoubtedly rank high among beneficial forms of entertainment and education. Entertainment, on the other hand, will become more mobile, more portable, and more continuous as an environment which surrounds the individual at almost all times. The ever-present portable radio and in-flight motion pictures are examples of traveling entertainment or of entertaining travel. The net result of the stepped-up melding of travel and entertainment plus education ought to be a market for benefit systems of infinite variety, composed with essential simplicity in their individual modules yet subject to highly complex combinations and permutations depending on personal preference and needs as dictated by the changing variables of time and place.

Index